Merchandizing Prisoners

Who Really Pays for Prison Privatization?

Byron Eugene Price

PRAEGER

Westport, Connecticut
London

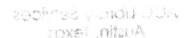

Library of Congress Cataloging-in-Publication Data

Price, Byron Eugene.
  Merchandizing prisoners: who really pays for prison privatization? / Byron Eugene Price.
     p. cm.
  Includes bibliographical references and index.
  ISBN 0–275–98738–8 (alk. paper)
  1. Prisons—United States. 2. Privatization—United States.
3. Corrections—Contracting out—United States. I. Title.
  HV9469.P745 2006
   365'.7—dc22   2005034805

British Library Cataloguing in Publication Data is available.

Library of Congress Catalog Card Number: 2005034805
ISBN: 0–275–98738–8

First published in 2006

Praeger Publishers, 88 Post Road West, Westport, CT 06881
An imprint of Greenwood Publishing Group, Inc.
www.praeger.com

Printed in the United States of America

The paper used in this book complies with the
Permanent Paper Standard issued by the National
Information Standards Organization (Z39.48–1984).

10 9 8 7 6 5 4 3 2 1

In memory of my brother Darryl A. Parks, born March 22, 1959 and departed this earth December 26, 2005. Rest in peace.

Contents

Illustrations

Tables

Figures

Acknowledgments

I would like to thank Marc Holzer, my department chair, for his leadership and support during this project. Thanks are due to Gabriela Kütting, Gerald Miller, Norma Riccucci, and John Baker for lending me their eyes, ears, time, and suggestions for how to improve this project. I would also like to thank John C. Morris, Edward J. Clynch, David A. Breaux, Melvin C. Ray, and Rick L. Travis for helping to shape this idea in its early stages. This manuscript benefited from the comments and suggestions of three anonymous referees. I am grateful to Melissa Rivera and Madelene Perez for making their word processing expertise available to me during the past year; I could not have completed this project in a timely manner if they had not put their work aside to help me with this manuscript. My graduate assistants, Wenxuan Yu and Rakhi Poonia, and Marlene Riley, the university's interlibrary loan specialist spent tireless days and nights in the library and before their computers conducting research for this manuscript; I am indebted to the three of them, and I could not have completed the project without their support. I would especially like to thank Gail Daniels for encouraging me to stay focused on this project while other projects threatened to swamp me. I am thankful to Vergil Ratliff and a host of other friends for helping me grow professionally, personally, and spiritually. Last but not least, I would like to especially thank my editor Suzanne Staszak-Silva for having confidence in me and this project. Her comments and suggestions were extremely helpful, and the project would not have been completed without her dedication.

This book is dedicated to my mother Mable E. Price, whose love helped us rise above poverty—"you are the wind beneath my wings." I would like to also dedicate this book to my oldest sister Joycelyn A. Parks; I thank her for keeping us out of harm's way while mother was away working. Thanks for always supporting your little brother. Thanks to my big brother Darryl A. Parks, who taught me how to be confident. Growing up in the projects with low self-esteem can be detrimental, but I overcame it because of the confidence he imparted to me. Finally, I would like to thank my youngest sister Linda F. Price for understanding and supporting me when no one else did as a child. Your support has been a blessing.

Introduction

A question that continues to compel the public policy community is: "Why do state policy makers privatize their prisons?" The conventional response by political and appointed policy leaders has consistently and unequivocally been that it is to reduce costs. This answer appeals to taxpayers, of course, who often take such justifications at face value.[1]

The truth driving a state's decision to privatize may, in fact, be quite different. This book examines the potential determinants of state prison privatization across the United States. In particular, it asks whether states are driven more by financial concerns, such as the private sector's ability to deliver superior savings and services, or by ideological and political factors.

The demand for prison cells in the United States began to grow in the mid- to late '70s for a variety of reasons. Two particularly salient reasons were increased rates of immigration detention and a dramatic rise in violent crimes, such as murder, rape, and robbery, especially in urban centers. In response to the need for new prison cells, state and federal legislatures across the United States enacted criminal sentencing reforms that stiffened penalties meted out to criminals. At the same time, the war on drugs increased the prison population by large numbers and resulted in longer sentences.

As a consequence of these factors, an arduous campaign was undertaken to build prisons to meet the growing demand of the burgeoning prisoner population. Capacity, however, was never able to keep up with demand. Studies conducted by independent for-profit agencies such as Abt Associates, as well as by the National Institute of Justice, found that by 1995 governments still had not brought supply in line with demand for prisoners incarcerated.[2] The inevitable outcome was prison overcrowding, which created a combustible environment for prisons by adding increased tension to an institution already susceptible to eruption by any incident. The courts responded by ruling that the deficient confinement conditions comprised a violation of the Eighth Amendment's prohibition of cruel and unusual punishment. Courts decreed that states must address the overcrowding conditions immediately. According to one report, "by 1988, prisons and jails in thirty-nine states, plus the District of Columbia, US Virgin Islands, and Puerto Rico were under such court orders."[3] The growing prison population and the federal court orders wreaked havoc on states' budgets, which forced an increase in spending.

Beginning in the mid-1980s, the privatization of jails and prisons grew considerably in the United States. Not only was there a steady growth of private, for-profit operations of federal, state, and county correctional facilities but private firms also became more involved in other aspects of the prison industry, such as the financing and construction of new prisons and the renovation of existing ones. Moreover, many of these private companies (for example, Wackenhut Corrections) went public and began trading on the stock exchanges.[4] As a result of government efforts, "perhaps more so than with other service industries in this country, the privatization of prisons has become a growth industry."[5]

Prison privatization continues to be one of the most controversial issues in public policy. Although steeped in "public choice" rationalizations to save costs through competitive bidding, privatization may also be rooted in the sociopolitical atmosphere that emerged from the antigovernment populism of the Reagan presidency. The privatization of prisons has led not only to significant changes in policy making and the management of prisons but also has generated widespread concerns that incarceration has become a profit-making industry strengthened by calls for policies, such as mandatory minimum sentencing, that would keep the prison industry growing.

In fact, the initial research for this book found evidence that the desire to save costs *may not be* the primary reason why states privatize their prisons. Rather, I found that the more plausible explanations revolve around political and ideological factors, such as the party of the governor and the overall political and ideological culture of the state.

Chapter Organization

Chapter one explores the history, meaning, and viewpoints in debate surrounding prison privatization. Additionally, this chapter examines the forms of privatization and the broader issues in the privatization literature, such as the political nature of privatization. For many, the power to punish is an inherently public function, but supporters of prison privatization have managed to convince state agencies that they can manage prisons better than the state; thus, the move toward prison privatization in the late 1970s, mid-1980s, and 1990s was brisk. Finally, the chapter looks at arguments for and against prison privatization.

Chapter two examines the traditional reasons provided for why states seek prison privatization. States that privatize their prisons tend to explain their rationale from three points of view: economy and efficiency, effectiveness, and quality. Each argument attests that privatization is superior to public management. However, in the next chapter, it will become apparent that the standard explanations are inadequate to explain why states privatize. In addition, issues of abuse and accountability are discussed to determine if private providers offer superior management in all spheres, ranging from administrative and cost-effective functions to lawful prisoner care.

The chapter revisits many well-documented abuse cases in public and private prisons and explores the government's role in determining accountability when it abdicates its responsibility to a private entity—that is, when the government transfers the power to punish to contractors. The Abu Ghraib prison scandal has focused attention on the issue of ensuring contractors' accountability to the public. Many private agencies adopt polices that maximize the bottom line, but these policies may leave them vulnerable to potential problems such as abuse. The abuse and accountability issues, along with a critique of the claims of superiority made by private prisons, are scrutinized more closely in this chapter because they are directly relevant to the privatization debate.

Chapter three provides a framework to examine the move toward prison privatization and explains empirical findings that contradict many of the claims states have made to explain why they sought prison privatization. The framework to study prison privatization consists of a consideration of economic, ideological, and political factors. The explanations for states' privatization in chapter three expand on those in chapter two, looking at the decision to privatize from a more complex perspective. For instance, the economic health of the state, the business cycle, and the need for prison labor were found to be possible explanations for prison privatization; however, the ideological variables concerning prison privatization were found to be very prominent in state-level decision-making as well. In addition, this chapter demonstrates how the "get tough on crime" and "war on drugs" campaigns orchestrated by conservatives served as a tool to foster privatization of prisons for the sake of securing profits for a few well-connected politicians. The current number of people incarcerated in the United States bears out this fact.

Chapter four explores the role speculative prisons play in shaping decision-making and demonstrates the underlying economic incentives inherent in management of private prisons. Speculative prisons are prisons built by for-profit prisons without state involvement. These prisons are built to take advantage of the states' overcrowding problems and the citizens' resistance to using bonds to build a new prison. For-profit prison providers recognized the business opportunity overcrowding problems and citizens' tax resistance presented to them, and they proceeded to build these prisons; private businesses do not need the state's permission to build a facility as long as they meet building and inspection ordinances. However, there was a certain degree of risk associated with building speculative prisons because of the possibility that the state would not use the facility. The chapter also investigates how private providers or entrepreneurs looked at a state's fiscal problems, crime rate, and overcrowding problems and determined that the state could use another prison and then built prisons without the state's involvement on a speculative basis.

These entrepreneurs target rural communities with high unemployment figures and convince them that private prisons are a great economic development tool to revitalize their community. The argument for economic development is a convincing argument; according to a 2001 report by Good Jobs First, "at least 73% of private prisons received a development subsidy from local, state and/or federal government sources."[6]

The speculative prison acts as an incentive to residents considering the depressed state of their communities and the state's willingness to subsidize the prisons. Also important when considering speculative prisons is the space-utilization theory or the cliché "build them and they will come." Private agencies that manage prisons go as far as soliciting other states for prisoners when there is a downward turn in the crime rate and the respective state has no prisoners to send to the private agencies. For instance, Youngstown, Ohio, has imported prisoners from Washington DC, and Hawaii has exported prisoners to Texas because the state could not afford or was unwilling to build additional prisons. There are certain rhetorical questions that must be posed because of these practices, which this manuscript attempts to answer. For instance, what are the implications of importing and exporting prisoners? What are the implications when these prisons are built and the crime rate goes down? Are private agencies likely to lobby states to allow them to import prisoners? Will they lobby for mandatory sentencing and other stiffer sentences? States that allow private agencies to build these types of prisons assume a great deal of risk. When the prison does not bring the necessary jobs promised or there are not enough prisoners to fill the beds, does the state begin to look for ways to secure prisoners to meet its contractual obligations? In others words, does the state become more punitive in its sentencing policies to meet its per diem obligation to the private agency?

As stated, when a prison has been built, states are forced to use the existing facility because state officials cannot justify to taxpayers why a new prison should be built using public funds when one is available that was built with funds many believe to be private. This chapter explores this aspect of prison privatization along with what is being done to regulate speculative prisons.

Chapter five examines the perceived economic incentives that underlie prison privatization. Because for-profit prison stock is publicly traded, there appears to be a vested interest in incarceration. As a result, private providers of prisons may attempt to influence criminal justice policy by making campaign contributions to lawmakers in hopes that they will support the stringent correctional policies these corporations advocate. From chapter three, there is evidence that this may actually reflect what is taking place in this industry.

This chapter also addresses another concern: Should the state give the right to punish to a private entity, especially one that potentially benefits from punishment? Because private prisons trade on the stock exchange, are they more interested in profits than rehabilitation, as alleged? Considering that private providers lobby for stiffer sentences and other punitive laws to keep prisoners longer, it would seem that they are more interested in profits. This chapter explores this aspect of prison privatization along with the use of prison labor and the economic incentives inherent in the growing prison industrial complex, such as the growing crime industry attendant on the growth of private prisons and the corrections-commercial complex.

Some have asserted that prison privatization in the United States is an extension of Jim Crow laws, which were very popular before the civil rights movement. Under this system, African Americans were deprived of life, liberty, and freedom. Opponents of privatization argue that private prisons do not protect the basic human rights of these individuals under their care. For instance, it is alleged that prisoners are abused and beaten more often in private prisons than public prisons. Under Jim Crow laws, African Americans had no right to sell their labor; however, after emancipation, they began to compete in a desegregated labor market. As a result, employment opportunities became more competitive. With diminishing opportunities for whites in the employment market, segregationists began to devise ways to circumvent the newly acquired rights of African Americans and to recapture their cheap—or better yet, free—labor. White leaders in the South began to target certain crimes that African Americans were most likely to commit, such as vagrancy, to imprison them for the purpose of reclaiming cheap labor. The convict lease system was devised under this new system of slavery—imprisonment. Convicts were leased out to private agencies, and the state was paid their wages for the work they performed.

This chapter explores in depth the economic incentives that are considered alongside prison privatization and the political implications, such as felony disenfranchisement, to see if private prisons are used to re-enslave African Americans to recapture cheap labor and to disenfranchise a growing minority that could possibly alter the election map if fully enfranchised.

Chapter six scrutinizes current trends in state practices concerning prison privatization to see if the move to privatize prisons has increased, stayed about the same, or decreased. Additionally, the chapter examines state actions to see if any states are following Mississippi's lead in breaking existing contracts with private prison vendors to help serious budget woes. This chapter also considers the fact that a state cannot guarantee prisoners to vacant prisons because many are facing a decreasing crime rate. Furthermore, with Mississippi's budget problems, the private providers cannot expect the state to continue to pay a per diem when the prisons have no prisoners; as a result, Mississippi is canceling contracts with private agencies that run the private prisons. This chapter looks at the current status of prison privatization and its future. Moreover, the chapter examines the prevailing issues and problems that exist with prison privatization today and the implications for prison privatization: What is the future of prison privatization, and how will it play out in the face of the extant problems?

Finally, the chapter looks at how economics and politics intersect and help shape decision-making. In addition, the chapter looks at interest groups, public employee unions, political culture, political aspirations, fiscal realities, and the struggle to determine how services will be provided for the states in the future and the role they play in the face of tax-resistant citizens.

Chapter One

States and the Prison Privatization Debate

Introduction

The debate regarding whether privatization is a viable option to alleviate inefficiency, red tape, and monopoly conditions associated with the public sector is a partisan debate, with public-sector employees, unions, and pro-privatizers situated right in the middle of the fracas. Public-sector employees and unions provide compelling evidence that contradicts the claims made by supporters of prison privatization that they can mange and operate prisons better; however, supporters of prison privatization provide just as much compelling evidence. Because both parties provide substantial evidence to support their positions, I attempt to look at their claims impartially. I should add that I believe that, in some instances, privatization is a viable option to alleviate fiscal stress; however, I do believe overall that prisons, the military, and police departments are inherently public functions and should remain publicly managed. Privatizing prison food services or health services is one thing, but the management of prisons should remain the states' responsibility because there is an added incentive to incarcerate once the prison becomes privatized.

Although I do take the position that prison privatization, in general, is a bad idea, it is not because my livelihood depends on whether or not a prison is privatized. I have no stake in the argument other than to advocate for a better system for communities, government, correction departments, and society at large. What is interesting about this debate is that it has been with us for some time, and I suspect it is here to stay.

Historical Overview of Prison Privatization

Privatization has been around before the 1980s and can be traced to ancient times if we consider contracting out as a form of privatization.[1] It has been found that, "for example, contracting out was tried as a tool of administration for provision of public services and for governmental performance under Darius the Great during the Persian world-state Achaemenid Empire (559–330 BC), in which two financial banking houses in the Babylonian Satrapy, Marashu & Sons and Egibi (one Persian and Jewish), were contracted out by the state for collecting fixed property taxes."[2] Furthermore, Greek mercenaries were contracted out to fight in the Persian army. The mercenaries were also contracted out under the aegis of the Persian army to do major public works, such as irrigation canals, bridges, and more.[3]

Having a history, although not a stellar one, in the public sector not only helped facilitate the privatization movement but also served as an impetus for the privatization of correctional services. The National Prison Congress of 1870, held in Cincinnati, Ohio, escorted in a new epoch in the administration of penal institutions. Along with this new era came a stress on vocational training and prisoner labor. One legacy of the First National Prison Congress of 1870, which laid the groundwork for the current prison environment, was the idea that prison was an industry and should be operated as such—efficiently and for profit.[4]

The idea that prisons would be run as an industry was a godsend for the South because of the hardships brought about as a result of the Civil War. The economy of the South was ravaged by the Civil War, and a byproduct of this economic instability was that many southern states did not have the financial wherewithal to operate a penal institution. As a result, states with little resources, like Mississippi in 1866, decided to award a fourteen-year lease to a private firm to operate their state prisons. Prisons in Huntsville, Texas, were at one time leased to a private entrepreneur.[5] In the mid-1800s, economizing state legislatures awarded contracts to private entrepreneurs to operate and manage Louisiana's first state prison, New York's Auburn and Sing Sing penitentiaries, and others.[6] The privatization of correctional facilities took hold; other states followed these models, and private prisons became the norm later in the century.

Imprisonment first surfaced in the post-war South as the overriding method of punishment because of a need to exploit and train captive labor that, as a result of the emancipation of slaves, was no longer available. Other countries use imprisonment as a main punishment, too, but they don't have the recent slave labor history.[7] A dearth of laborers served as the impetus for the modern prison because of its role in training and exploiting labor reserves; thus we have the invention of the convict leasing system and chain gangs, which were still in existence in Alabama up until 1995. Although the prison system has undergone reform on many occasions, the penal philosophy has always had a leaning toward the punitive rather than the rehabilitative and restitutive.

The dominant penal philosophy, which developed in the late 1970s and early 1980s, continues to be conservative and punitive. The "just desserts" model, as it has been termed, utilizes the "social contract" concept to justify punishment of those who break the law. It promotes the idea that the only goal of the justice system should be justice, not reform of the individual.[8] However, the National Institute of Law Enforcement and Criminal Justice disagrees with this assertion, contending that the criminal justice system has, from the late 1970s to the present day, reconstituted itself as far as its purpose is concerned by moving toward broadening and expanding the meaning, scope, and procedure for carrying out penal sanctions imposed by society on criminals.[9] For instance, some states use drug courts and boot camps to divert first time and nonviolent offenders from prisons. This has not always been true.

Some researchers maintain that no other variable has been more important in privatization than economic forces.[10] I support this assertion by contending that the proponents have argued that demand and supply of economic systems in capitalism have improved to the benefit of consumers who have enough money to pay for public goods and services; the welfare state once considered imperative for the system no longer has a role in the system.[11]

American Friends Service Committee notes that this shift, as it concerned how criminals should be dealt with, was also expressed by liberal and conservative social scientists, criminologists, and other scholars as they began to voice the opinion that rehabilitation did not work.[12] This trend initiated a shift toward the right and, "it signaled that imprisonment for retribution and deterrence, rather than rehabilitation, was more acceptable."[13]

The move from the focus being on rehabilitation to one of retribution facilitated a new view on how criminals should be punished. The impetus behind this shift was the perceived failure of the "war on poverty," which sought to attack crime through social engineering. Because the social engineering era of the "war on poverty" was perceived as such a dismal failure in mitigating the impact of crime, the public's patience with rehabilitation also turned and they became more hostile toward rehabilitation for criminals. As a result, the public felt that punishment should be swift and unforgiving to effectively deter future lawbreakers; thus determinate sentencing replaced indeterminate sentencing, and mandatory sentencing laws began to make their way back onto the books. The consensus in this period was that it would be cheaper for society in the long run to increase the use of imprisonment. The conservative change was the galvanizing force in the penal shift that took place in the United States, coupled with an insatiable public appetite for law and order, which eventually resulted in an unprecedented number of imprisoned offenders during the 1980s and early 1990s;[14] thus, the initial momentum for privatization was a result of public opinion, especially conservative orientations and pressures placed on politicians by the public to do something about high crime rates.

Faced with rapidly growing correctional budgets and shrinking resources, states have sought out creative and innovative financing arrangements for new prison construction to alleviate the pressures being placed on budgets by growing correctional expenditures. The think tank Research Roundup asserts that one strategy that was being used more and more by states during the height of privatization, although it was a very controversial solution, was the creation of privately constructed, privately managed facilities.[15] The states' need to alleviate pressures imposed by increasing costs of incarceration, which have allowed the movement to privatize correctional institutions to gain considerable momentum.[16] On the other hand, scholars contend that the interest in privatization is prompted partly by the concern

> that the federal government has become too large, too expensive, and too intrusive in our lives. The interest also reflects a belief that new arrangements between the government and the private sector might improve efficiency while offering new opportunities and greater satisfaction for the people served.[17]

Opponents of privatization profess that prisons and prison operations have historically been the province of the government and should remain so.[18] They imply that our prisons are publicly managed due to our early negative experiences with the management practices of private entities. This idea is reinforced by the experiences of states that have used private prisons in the past, such as California, Louisiana, Michigan, Oklahoma, and Texas. These states had privately operated prisons between 1850 and 1950. The prisoners were farmed out to the private sector administrators as individual servants or to businesses operated by the same administrators. The money resulting from prisoner labor helped maintain the correctional systems. By 1950, the situation came to a head, and privately managed prisons came to an end after it was discovered that there was rampant prisoner abuse in these prisons. However, correctional privatization appears to rise from the ashes like a phoenix. The latest rebirth happened in 1979, when the U.S. Immigration and Naturalization Service (INS) began contracting with private firms to detain illegal immigrants and the privatization movement in corrections began to reappear. But the actual proliferation occurred during the 1980s due to the problem with expanding prison populations, pressures from courts to quickly add prison space, and increases in prison costs, which the Government Accounting Office (GAO) asserts rekindled interest in using privately managed prisons.[19]

Questions concerning whether prisons should be reprivatized began to arise. Most of the debate centered on whether or not the government should or could legally contract a private prison without breaching the "social contract." The right of society to punish has its roots in the philosophy of the social contract. This idea gained its greatest currency during the Age of Enlightenment in the seventeenth and eighteenth centuries and is associated with Thomas Hobbes, John Locke, and Jean-Jacques Rousseau.[20] In essence, the concept captures Locke's idea from his *Second Treatise on Government*: "government derives its power from the consent of the governed."

As the public and various legislative bodies looked for reasons to justify prison privatization, the social contract provided the justification to appease their conscience concerning privatizing what many believe is an inherently public function. No longer concerned with justifying privatizing corrections, nineteenth-century state legislators realized that turning the correctional system over to the private sector could be an advantageous cost-cutting opportunity. Factors that influenced their decisions to solicit private involvement in corrections were overcrowding problems, costs to the state, the general economic well-being of the respective states, and the demise of the slave economy, especially in the South. Contrary to the perspective of most observers, privatization of corrections is far from a modern innovation. The nineteenth century was an epoch of intense involvement of the private industry in the implementation of correctional services. As privately run prisons reached their zenith in the late nineteenth century, allegations began to surface concerning corruption and prisoner abuse. The allegations carried enough weight and eventually led to the total discontinuance of for-profit penal institutions by the middle of the twentieth century.

In a number of studies, scholars have acknowledged the past problems with prison privatization and the possible problems that may occur in reconsidering privatization, but most contemporary studies assert that it is worth the effort to reprivatize prisons.[21] Most studies link the contemporary consideration of prison privatization to prison overcrowding, conservative ideology, and polemics over cost-efficiency and management concerns. According to an article in the journal *Crime, Law and Social Change*, "the renewed interest in privatization of corrections contains some unique features: (a) it includes the privatization of the management of entire prisons. (b) Modern correctional privatization is being done by firms, which have been formed specifically for this purpose (for example Corrections Corporation of America, Buckingham) or are specialized subsidiaries of large corporations (for example RCA, Westinghouse, General Electric, Wackenhut)."[22] On the other hand, the American Federation of State, County, and Municipal Employees (AFSCME) and other opponents of prison privatization are concerned about the renewed interest in correctional privatization. If prisons become an attractive investment option to the public, the public may become more amenable to private prisons; this would erode AFSCME's ability to lobby against private prisons, which would eventually threaten their jobs.[23]

Unlike today, firms responsible for private prisons of the past did not offer shares to investors trading on the stock exchange. Many critics of correctional privatization assert that stock prices have led to the current problems that plague the industry. Opponents of correctional privatization also contend that the well-documented problems with private prisons during the nineteenth and earlier twentieth century should not be forgotten and decision-makers should be more prudent before they turn over the right to punish to an entity that has an apparent vested interest in punishment. For instance, contemporary decision-makers should consider that private adult corrections during the nineteenth and early twentieth century disappeared under the pressure of prisoner abuse scandals, labor union opposition, and job scarceness in the Great Depression. Critics assert that the profit motive served as the impetus for this abuse. The introduction of the profit motive to corrections served as a pioneering modification in the early nineteenth century prisons, and the outlook on corrections has never been the same since. Once the profit motive was introduced into corrections, the prison as an industry was created. This meant that the investment of private capital and the daily involvement of private entrepreneurs or their representatives in the affairs of prisons would forever be a part of the landscape.[24]

It is suggested that the liberal Progressive Era was responsible for the emergence of the federal police and a flood of prison building.

After World War II, there seemed to be a synthesis between the liberals and conservatives who both wanted to use criminal justice extensively—liberals to rehabilitate criminals and conservatives to control them. Both wanted to increase criminal justice involvement—but for different reasons. Since the 1980s and the Reagan administration, there has been a growing conservatism in America. Even the liberals can be described as having moved to the right. A desire to downsize the government has accompanied this shift. While most are reluctant to credit that desire to criminal justice—witness the growth of federal criminal justice in all areas—the current privatization movement is part of that response.[25] Much of the impetus for industry growth came from Tennessee Republican activist Thomas Beasley, who founded Corrections Corporation of America (CCA) in 1983 in Nashville, Tennessee, with backing from venture capitalist Jack Massy, who also helped build Kentucky Fried Chicken and Hospital Corporation of America.[26] After its inception, a contract was awarded to CCA in 1984 in Hamilton County, Tennessee, to completely operate the jail. With this contract, the beginning of the modern-day private prison business was born. In 1985, CCA proffered to take over the entire Tennessee prison system for $200 million. Although CCA was unsuccessful in its bid to take over the entire Tennessee prison system, they have grown and are estimated to control 50 percent of the private prison market. In addition, for-profit prison revenues have surpassed the $1 billion mark as of 1998.[27] Their bank accounts are not the only growth they have experienced; for instance, by 1999 there were twelve for-profit firms across the United States with more than half of the for-profit prisons located in four states: Texas (43), California (24), Florida (10), and Colorado (9).[28]

During the late 1970s and enduring through the 1980s, many federal, state, and local governments began to express a great deal of interest in private corrections as a result of a new receptivity to incarceration, which was galvanized by politicians who spanned the entire political continuum. Additionally, their interest was intensified by an increase in crime rates and a discouraging lack of rehabilitation results. Political frustration with this situation, coupled with a cynical public view toward the ability of the government to reduce crime, fueled the imprisonment binge.[29] This new period of incarceration led to an expansion in the prison population and, as a result, escalated the costs of corrections by excessive proportions. Not cost, frustration, nor fear alone can be said to have created the penal enigma described; instead, these factors, combined with an era of government downsizing and economic instability, brought privatization of corrections to the vanguard.[30] The Grace Commission, initiated by President Reagan, created the climate in the 1980s for the reconsideration of privatization as a solution to public problems. The privatization theme was the driving force behind the Reagan administrative theory of government and hence market economics.[31] The Grace Commission's recommendations were a vehicle used by the Reagan administration to reach the objective of increased private-sector involvement in the production and/or provision of government services; the commission also served as one of the strongest initiatives ever taken by an administration toward reaching the goal of privatization.[32]

Long-term imprisonment has become a common practice in the United States since the 1970s.[33] Coupled with prisoner crowding, the prohibitive cost of maintaining correctional facilities has resulted in a search for alternative practices designed to assuage the financial burden placed on state and federal correctional systems.[34]

The cry of taxpayers that governments provide more services with fewer resources gained currency in the political and economic context of the 1980s.[35] This movement to privatize public services has received growing support as taxpayers have demanded that government provide more services with fewer resources. Advocates of correctional privatization often argue from a "public choice" theoretical perspective, as do most proponents of privatization. The majority assert that private organizations can provide correctional services at a lower cost than governmental agencies.[36] The theory that less government is better is a tenet of public choice, which is the "economic study of non-market decision-making, or merely the application of economic methodology to study questions customarily examined by political science."[37] Advocates of public choice use the economic issues that adversely impact states as one of the reasons states should privatize corrections.

The early 1980s were marked by vigorous and rancorous debate regarding the propriety of escalating private sector involvement in the correctional system. Supporters of privatization argued that private industry could take on accountability for various aspects of the penal system with greater managerial efficiency, resulting in cost savings.[38] Such cost claims are of special interest in lieu of the rapidly increasing prison population.[39] This is substantiated by the Bureau of Justice Statistics, which reports that the prison population more than doubled in the 1980s, exceeding 800,000 prisoners.[40]

As stated earlier, privatization is not new to corrections, and one of the earliest examples noted in the literature is the fee for services system in American jails. These fees were collected from prisoners or their families to provide for salaries of the sheriff and jailer. The explosion in prison and jail populations has led to a building boom in corrections. According to a chapter in the book *Privatizing Correctional Institutions,* "the building boom, coupled with the inability of state and local government to finance the needed new construction through traditional methods such as general obligation bond issues or higher taxes, has encouraged the entry of private investment firms into the area of correctional facility financing."[41] Crowding and the cost associated with a burgeoning prison population are relevant factors in the modern privatization debate and are the main arguments made for privatization as they were in the 1800s.

Research shows that there are four main issues in the privatizations of prisons:

- Can private prisons saves public revenues by doing it cheaper?

- Is accountability lost when the state contracts with a private company?

- Are prisons inherently a public function and not suited for privatization?

- Does privatization "result in a loss of capacity on the part of the state to deliver an important service"?[42]

Other criticisms of privatization claim that, by privatizing public services, the government risks not being able to respond to public needs, especially when only two private agencies control 74 percent of the prisons.[43] What happens if they go bankrupt? This could have serious consequences for cash-strapped governments trying to respond to a situation that requires them to dig deeper into their coffers to either bail out the companies or take over the prisons themselves. However, governments are provided with another option—to find another private entity to take over the facility. The likelihood of achieving this goal is feasible because CCA and Wackenhut (now known as the Geo Group) have the resources to step in and take over the prisons. But, does the government want two agencies that control 74 percent of the market to end up controlling 100 percent of the market? If the answer were yes, this would constitute a monopoly. If this were to happen, for-profit prison firms would no longer be able to argue that they foster competition as a reason for privatization. They would be guilty of creating the same climate of which they accuse the government—monopoly conditions.

Privatization Climate

Prison privatization has become one of the most controversial issues in public policy. Fiscal pressures, increased correctional costs, and prison overcrowding coagulated and led to health issues and increased violence in prisons, which highlighted the importance of the prison privatization issue to the public. Stringent correctional policies, such as mandatory sentencing, truth-in-sentencing, and longer sentences, have also added to the fiscal woes of states. Coupled with the conservative "get tough on crime" climate ushered in by the Reagan administration, prison overcrowding threatened to bankrupt states. As a result, states struggled with decisions about how to fund policies and programs such as education and infrastructure in the face of an ailing economy. The budget problems of states became more pronounced due to the economic slowdown of the late twentieth century. States were pressed to make difficult funding decisions to meet public demands for services.

The cooling economy in conjunction with the overcrowding problems made it more difficult for states to implement policies that improved the lives of citizens on a daily basis. The problem became so severe for the state of Mississippi that it cut the education budget, which resulted in a lack of pay raises for employees at institutions of higher learning across the state for three years. Mississippi was not alone in its budgets problems; state budgets across the nation were affected because of the increased correctional costs concomitant with the "get tough on crime" and the "war on drugs" campaigns. Some were even threatened with insolvency if an immediate solution was not found to avert the burden being placed on budgets by corrections. Courts facilitated the move toward privatization when they mandated that states address the overcrowding problems by enabling legislation that allowed states to contract with private corporations to privatize prisons.

As states faced these issues head-on, many opted for alternative solutions, such as privatization, to address the problems presented by corrections. This transition from states being unwilling to privatize functions to being more amenable to privatizing public sector functions was observed during the national elections of 1978 and 1980, which revealed a change in public attitudes toward a greater role for the private sector in American life.

The belief that privatization is a response to the fiscal panic in the 1980s is ill-conceived because scholars also looked at the private delivery of public services as an option during the 1970s.[44] Less government involvement has always been a popular option; because of the American taste for free enterprise, there has always been a bias toward the private alternative.[45]

The real momentum for privatization and contracting began in the early 1980s with the big push by the conservative Right under American President Ronald Reagan and British Prime Minister Margaret Thatcher.[46] Both leaders vigorously advocated selling off government assets and reducing the government's role in the economy. According to John Donahue's book *The Privatization Decision: Public Ends, Private Means*, "privatization, as today's fiscally ambitious, ideologically charged phenomenon, began as a British import."[47] As the British shed major assets and responsibilities throughout the 1980s,[48] conservative intellectuals in the United States set out to emulate the British example.[49]

Well-respected conservatives in the United States began to publish books, government reports, and position papers promoting the benefits of privatization. Most of the literature reinforced Reagan's advocacy of privatization. President Reagan was not satisfied with promoting privatization; he was interested in permanently reducing the scope and role of government. To accomplish this task, he created the Grace Commission, which for all intents and purposes was formed to dismantle government. The Grace Commission recommended that the federal payroll be cut by half a million jobs—roughly one-sixth of the workforce—through contracting out governmental functions. With the stage set for privatization, privatization proposals by well-connected conservatives began to flow and, in 1985, culminated in a publication entitled "Privatizing Federal Spending: A Strategy to Eliminate the Deficit," by Heritage Foundation director Stuart M. Butler.[50]

The call to privatize appears to have resonated with the public; increasingly, government functions are being turned over to the private sector, including prisons, health care, wastewater management, and garbage collection. The move to privatize was strengthened with the Republican sweep of the 1994 midterm congressional elections and their publication of the "Contract with America." Both events cemented conservative support for privatization as a means to reduce the size and scope of government activity.[51] Since the 1970s, the interest in the privatization of public services in western industrialized countries has developed and increased significantly with the perpetual calls to reduce the scope of government. During the 1980s, interest again spiked in support of privatization and reducing the scope of government when conservative social policy and the political climate proved propitious to the reduction of functions of government in the face of fiscal demands.

The Meaning of Privatization

There are four strategic forms of privatization: contracting out (or outsourcing), vouchers, sale of assets, and load shedding.[52] In the United States, the primary type of privatization is contracting out, and it is spread across all levels of government. Of the four forms of privatization, it is also the most common arrangement a government pursues under a privatization agreement.

As stated, the trend for many governments has been to transfer or relocate responsibility for a range of public services to the private sector.[53] Increasing correctional expenditures and the "get tough on crime" and "war on drugs" campaigns forced governments to transfer services such as corrections and health care to for-profit firms in the interest of reducing fiscal stress. In the 1990s in the United States, most local governments had sought some type of privatization arrangement, while the federal government and state governments were more reluctant to embrace privatization.

The concept of privatization includes, but is not limited by, the following characteristics:

1. Governmental disconnection from a function, as in the termination of a program

2. The sale or lease of assets, such as land, infrastructure, or state-owned enterprises (SOEs)

3. The substitution of publicly produced services with public payments for private services through contracts, vouchers, etc.

4. Various forms of deregulation that open up an industry to private competition where previously public institutions were the only legal providers[54]

Of the four types of arrangements, outsourcing is the most common privatization arrangement in the correctional setting, and correctional privatization has assumed a number of institutional characteristics.[55] The National Council on Crime and Delinquency reports that "over the past two decades, the practice of state and local correctional agencies contracting with private entities for medical, mental health, educational, food services, maintenance, and administrative office security functions has risen sharply."[56] Under outsourcing arrangements, the correctional agency maintains control over policy decisions and the quality of service provided by the private agency, using a monitor to maintain policy control and management of the private facility.

In the 1980s and 1990s, there was an aggressive movement by prisons and juvenile facilities to use private vendors to supply a host of services, including food, health, counseling, vocational training, education, and, at times, administrative services. As a result of this new emphasis on privatizing the public sector, no area of government has been immune to privatization. For conservatives, privatization is desirable in any form, but for some liberals, philosophically this is synonymous to the government vacating its responsibility.

Proponents of privatization assert that when the government decides to contract out a public service or to privatize, it does not give up its financial support responsibility but employs a private company to provide the service. Supposedly, the primary motivations for many governments to contracting out are to reduce government costs by using more economically efficient private vendors and to allow public agencies to take advantage of the efficiency and specialized skills believed to be offered by the private sector that may be unavailable in the public sector. The private sector is believed to be more efficient than the government in performing commercial activities because the private firms are profit-driven.

Moreover, implicit in the discourse on privatization is the view shared by many scholars that the public and private sectors are both subject to the same set of economic incentives and disincentives.[57] Some advocates of privatization go as far as contending that nearly all public sector activities are potentially amenable to being transferred to the private sector.[58]

Another impetus for the increased use of privatization in state governments was the unparalleled devolution of public programs and responsibilities from Washington. Devolution stimulated inexorable pressures for smaller, less bureaucratic government from the grass roots and made states more amenable to the concept of privatization and the tools through which privatization could be brought to fruition.

The earliest years of the 1980s found state administrators buffeted by ideologically driven debates declaring privatization as the universal remedy for all governmental ills on the one hand and as anathema to sound government on the other; however, at the decade's

close, state privatization discussions shifted to a decidedly more pragmatic plane, free of the decade's dogmatism.[59]

The Case for Prison Privatization

During the apex of the prison privatization movement, it was
believed that the shift toward privatized corrections was mostly
driven by budgetary concerns. A report by an independent agency
appears to substantiate this widely held belief. The report found that
federal and state officials sought privatization to ameliorate the overcrowding in public prisons and to obtain additional prison beds.[60] The
move toward prison privatization was energized by advocates of
prison privatization who began to amplify states' fiscal fears by promising that they could manage prisons more cheaply, build them faster,
and operate them better.

The case for privatization also includes other declarations besides
improved efficiency and budget savings. The operative word is *choice*.
According to advocates for privatization, choice fosters competition
because public prisons currently operate under monopolistic conditions; this is why they are inefficient. Therefore, choice results in costs
savings because private operators are competing for their services.

Another claim of supporters of privatization is that the private sector can finance, construct, service, and operate most types of correctional facilities more efficiently than the government. These claims
are supported by a number of independent studies, which conclude
that private companies can finance new facilities without the need
for voter-approved bond issues and can construct them more quickly
and cheaply.[61] Other studies have found that private contractors,
freed from unwieldy public personnel policies and unionized work
forces are able to run correctional institutions and related programs
more efficiently and cheaply than their competitors, the public operators. This is also why private prison providers fight unionization.

The raison d'être generally provided for the superior performance
of the private sector is twofold. The first contention is that, "government lacks management flexibility because of union constraints on
decisions, which would reduce the number of workers, better using
existing capital."[62] A second reason is that the absence of competition

between government agencies creates a monopoly that eliminates the motivation to increase efficiency. Evidence from studies concerned with privatization does suggest that when an agency must compete with a contractor, its productivity can increase and even match the contractor's performance.

Another claim centers around the view that privatization is part of the formal political agenda as a function of problems encountered by governments at every level. In addition, gaping budget deficits and the seeming cost savings of privatization has lead to greater use of privatization. Proponents of privatization or public choice supporters claim that government participation has become too widespread and governments have certain characteristics that make successful correction of market failure extremely difficult, if not unlikely.

The amount of government involvement in the economy has always been the sticking point for those opposed to government intervention in the market. From the time of Adam Smith, the debate about government's role in the economy has been contentious. However, currently privatization's constituency continues to broaden, transcending both party boundaries and jurisdictional terrain, and can no longer be viewed as a conservative argument.[63] Further, privatization efforts are being vigorously pursued, even led, by Democratic as well as Republican governors and legislators and are reproduced in the work of state agencies from Maine to Texas and from Maryland to California.[64]

The Case against Private Prisons

Scholars point out that the existence of public services is a function of the inability or unwillingness of the private sector to engage in particular activities (that is, market failures) thought necessary for the common good.[65] Moreover, "the privatization of these services cannot be assumed to result in greater efficiencies unless, of course, the federal government engages in subsidization and regulation."[66] This implies that cost accompanies the subsidization and regulation of private prisons and, without the two, it remains to be seen if private firms can manage prisons more cheaply without government's assistance.

On the other hand, as private providers seek to reduce the costs associated with managing private prisons to prove that they are far better at keeping costs down than public prisons, issues of profitability become more prominent for for-profit providers. Critics assert that for-profit providers of prisons will attempt to maximize prisoner populations through changes in public policy, such as lobbying for policies such as mandatory sentencing.[67] Laws like mandatory sentencing keep prisons full and increase the labor supply in the name of maximizing profits.

As states began to pass mandatory sentencing laws, they actually played into the hands of for-profit firms. The laws led to dwindling state budgets, rising correctional costs, and prison overcrowding, which, in turn, has led to the current correctional crisis that exists today. The correctional crisis for states in the 1980s and 1990s centered on how to manage bulging prison populations in the face of fiscal pressures. As a result, many states sought alternative means—chiefly privatization—to address budget issues.

Privatizing prisons has support from conservatives and public choice scholars on the grounds that the private sector can operate the prisons more efficiently and effectively. On the other hand, critics argue, there is not enough evidence to support that contention because of the many hidden costs accompanying the transfer of resources to a private entity. Critics see privatization as an attempt to reduce the role and scope of government, which they contend eventually threatens the public interest because it denies the citizens in a representative democracy from participating in the processes of government decision-making on issues that impact their quality of life. Locating a prison in a community without citizen input is one of those quality-of-life altering events.

Once prisons become private, citizens lose access to their records because for-profit firms refuse to disclose information that will help citizens determine their effectiveness in securing public safety. There are potential legal ramifications to not disclosing their records. By losing access to their records, citizens are locked out of the decision-making process and the policy process, especially as it concerns what kind of prisoners are being housed in the facilities and what is being done to protect the community. For instance, Youngstown, Ohio, had an arrangement with Washington DC to house medium-risk prisoners in its medium-security prison; however, DC sent Youngstown maximum-security prisoners. The prisoners from DC eventual murdered several other prisoners. The citizens in this community were unaware of the hardened prisoners that were shipped to Youngstown because the facility did not make this kind of information public.

Another concern of opponents of prison privatization is that they consider the incarceration of individuals to be deeply associated with the fundamental function of government, and this responsibility should not be turned over to a private entity. They further argue that a distinction must be made between the choice to punish and the administration of punishment. Under this line of reasoning, scholars assume it is perfectly acceptable to recognize the decision to punish an individual as the government's responsibility and equally acceptable to allow a private entity under governmental supervision to administer the punishment, that is, operate the prison—implying social contract theory.[68] One of the concerns raised by present critics of correctional privatization is that profit-motivated firms will make decisions that maximize profits at the expense of the rights and well-being of prisoners. For instance, they point to the relationship between legislative members and for-profit administrators who are members of the American Legislative Exchange Council (ALEC) Criminal Justice Task Force Committee, which is responsible for authoring many of the laws state legislatures debate. Advocates counter by arguing that abusive practices would not be in the long-term interest of private contractors. However, this argument is not tenable because there are numerous documented cases of abuse that have taken place in for-profit prisons. For instance, critics point to the infamous incident in Brazoria, Texas, in which a guard was captured on tape dragging a prisoner across the floor, announced a welcome to Texas and said, "Enjoy the ride. It's like Astroworld."[69]

The question that arises is this: why have for-profit firms continued to flourish given their past egregious acts and their present problems? The answer may lie in the fact that "privatization of correctional facilities is best understood as an amalgamation of government failure, market failure, and political incentives."[70] According to a report by the Stennis Institute of Government at Mississippi State

University, "Traditional analyses of privatization tend to concentrate primarily on government failure as the justification for privatization; few tend to focus on either potential market failures or the political incentives in place to encourage privatization in a particular policy area."[71]

Finally, the debate about privatization always winds up being a discussion about how privatization saves taxpayers money. Although this argument does not consider the hidden expenses of monitoring the prison, the claim has been heard so often that it is accepted as truth. Critics of prison privatization see an inherent conflict in this type of service: private prisons remain profitable by making sure that prison beds are filled, and if they benefit from beds being filled, then no incentive exists for private prisons to take any actions that might reduce the recidivism rate. Lowering the recidivism rate through educational programs and various rehabilitation programs would end up lowering future revenues for these private contractors. For-profit prisons have been criticized for not having enough rehabilitative programs—but these programs are not in the long-term interest of these institutions.

The argument to support privatization because it increases efficiency or saves money has not been settled. More research must take place before the claim is substantiated because the majority of the research from both sides is highly partisan and without validation. Once objective research is conducted, more can be learned about the benefits and disadvantages of prison privatization. Presently, this is not the case, and this manuscript attempts to provide a balanced perspective on the viability of prison privatization.

Privatization Summary

Economic, ideological, and political streams of thought guide the arguments for and against privatization. The economic arguments focus on the idea that privatization maximizes efficiency, reduces costs, and promotes equity and competition. The reason economic arguments appear to be more appealing than the ideological and political arguments is the fact that the economic arguments resonate with states suffering with fiscal problems.

Conservatives promote privatization because it introduces competition. For them, introducing privatization would insert market pressures into the correctional system, which they believe would help alleviate the fiscal stress that is a byproduct of public prison monopolies. However, they also see a zero-sum relationship between government and the economy—the larger the public sector, the smaller the private economy.[72] The more public spending we have, the less private savings and investment will be available.[73] This argument captures the ideological thrust behind the impetus to privatize, although it has an economic slant; that is the distinction between this argument and the argument made in the economic stream.

Political arguments mostly focus on the idea that, in the interest of maximizing profit, private corporations charged with operating prisons will maximize prisoner population through changes in public policy, such as increasing mandatory sentencing legislation.[74] This avenue of discussion moves the argument to a state-level assessment from the piecemeal discussion of privatization that normally takes place—efficiency, effectiveness, and quality. The decision to privatize is a complicated decision, and scholars point out "that the decision by policy makers to contract out the implementation of their policies to private entrepreneurs is, in short, at least as much a political decision as it is a managerial and financial one."[75]

In sum, privatization has economic, ideological, and political underpinnings. Although at times liberals have embraced the idea of privatization, it is mostly a conservative tenet grounded in public choice theories and transaction costs. The "Reagan Revolution," the 1994 midterm elections, and the "Contract with America" helped solidify the idea that government is the problem and paved the way for privatization initiatives.

Although the efficiency and effectiveness argument seems to be at the core of the decision to privatize prisons, the ever-growing prison population has been characterized as playing a significant role in driving the decision to privatize. This seems to be supported by recent statistics, which show that "the total number of prisoners under the jurisdiction of federal or state adult correctional authorities was 1,381,892 at year end 2000."[76] Of that number, 87,369 were held in private facilities at the end of 2000.[77] The number of prisoners held in private facilities continues to grow.

Chapter Two

Explaining Prison Privatization: A View from the States

Introduction

The arguments regarding the superiority of private prisons are made without the support of research, and it is ironic that such arguments are accepted as putative. States with private prisons have been persuaded that private prisons are more efficient and provide a bigger "bang for their buck" than public ones—this, along with greater effectiveness, is why they were encouraged to privatize in the first place. These states also embrace prison privatization because for-profit prisons are believed to provide better quality, which translates into improved services for the incarcerated. I have classified the three criteria states use to evaluate prison privatization—efficiency, effectiveness, and quality—as standard explanations, and they are referred to henceforth as such. Standard explanations explore the decision to privatize prisons from a micro perspective, which I believe is inadequate. Chapter three offers a much broader examination to explain the decision to privatize. I look at the additional factors that move beyond the standard explanations, which I believe support my assertion that standard explanations fall short in their effort to explain the motives for prison privatization. The pro and con arguments, in addition to the mounting evidence, help to support my claim that the standard explanations are inadequate in explaining the decisions to privatize prisons, and additional factors should be considered before accepting the claims that private prisons are superior to public prisons.

Efficiency, Effectiveness, and Quality: More for Your Money

Economic arguments in the standard explanations as well as in the state discussion both argue for the superiority of private prisons. The basis of this support is grounded in public choice theory and the tension that exits between conservative economists who favor laissez-faire economics and liberals who favor government involvement. The public choice theory has its roots in economics, and it applies economic supposition to the decision-making of voters, politicians, and government officials. Supporters of laissez-faire economics have championed public choice as the panacea for fiscal pressures placed on state budgets as a result of increased correctional expenditures. The increased expenditures are a byproduct of the move from indeterminate sentencing to determinate sentencing. Authors who argue that privatization provides the biggest "bang for the buck" contend that privatization is superior to government service for the following reasons:

- Private prisons are more able to maximize efficiency.
- Costs will be lowered once prisons are privatized.
- Private prisons can achieve economies of scale.
- Private firms have better management information systems.
- Privatization promotes efficiency, cost-effectiveness, and competition.
- Private facilities can improve performance because competition results in cost savings.

- Private prisons can make government services more cost-effective by opening up competing channels of information and introducing competitive pressures.

The basic argument under this model is that privatization is superior to government because it introduces competition. Furthermore, proponents argue that private facilities are less expensive because they are not mired in red tape versus public facilities; they are not hampered by unions and do not have to wait for the municipality to pass a bond issue.

Moreover, studies on prison privatization that attest to their ability to produce savings and operate for less money cite two primary reasons: "flexibility in their purchasing procedures and the incentive to reduce the cost of general supplies which is not present in a state agency; and staffing flexibility which allows private firms more flexibility in assigning work responsibilities because they are not hampered by union rules because they do not typically employ unionized workers and they accomplish the tasks without jeopardizing safety or quality."[1]

Support for the superiority of the private sector can be found in the teachings of Adam Smith (1723–1790), a Scottish professor of moral philosophy whose book *The Wealth of Nations* is one of the major original works on economic liberalism. His ideas are among the most prominent in shaping extant American socioeconomic philosophy, as well as being one of the major influences on Thatcher's economic policy, which in turn was a strong influence on the 1980s drive for privatization. He is considered to be the forefather of the pure liberal ideology that surfaced when the conventional social forces acquiesced to the ever-increasing political and economic power of the bourgeoisie.[2] Smith strongly opposed government interference or regulation and privileges for monopolies. He saw free competition as the most effective policy for government to pursue. According to this philosophy, a free unfettered economy will provide to every citizen a fair and equal chance to do what he or she does best. Smith argued that free competition among private enterprises would result in greater income for everyone.[3] However, the original argument by

Smith had a strong moral and social component, which Reagan and Thatcher let fall by the wayside in the pursuit of privatization.

In American culture, adjectives such as progress, productivity, and efficiency are associated with private enterprise, while inefficiency, stagnation, and corruption are attached to the public sector. This perception remains persistent even in today's social thought. For example, in the preface to the *Report of the President's Commission on Privatization*, its chairperson reinforces this belief by stating that:

> The American people have often complained of the intrusiveness of federal programs, of inadequate performance, and of excessive expenditures. In light of these public concerns, government should consider turning to the creative talents and ingenuity in the private sector to provide possible and appropriate better answers to present and future challenges.[4]

The theory that less government is better is a tenet of public choice, which is the "economic study of nonmarket decision-making, or merely the application of economic methodology to study questions customarily examined by political science."[5] Advocates of public choice use the economic issues that impact states adversely as one of the reasons states should privatize corrections.

Furthermore, privatization promotes efficiency, and it is economically efficient because private property rights provide motivation for cost-effectiveness; it is evenhanded to the extent that government enterprises are almost always accorded monopoly power by fiat.[6] Thinkers in this school believe that permitting services to be provided by private competitive enterprises eliminates monopoly power, thereby benefiting consumers and taxpayers.

Cost Savings Studies

There are reservations concerning the favorable cost reviews promoting the superiority of correctional privatization.[7] Cost is not the concern of those who draw on the spirit of Locke, Rousseau, and Hume; for them, punishment is an inherently public function. To remain valid and ethically meaningful, punishment must remain with the government, because when we deprive citizens of their liberty, the authority to govern behind bars must remain in the hands of government authorities; that is the only way punishment remains legitimate. This implies that states should be cautious about privatizing corrections. However, states have proceeded with correctional privatization despite admonishments from scholars.

States have pursued privatization of corrections despite taxpayer resistance in the form of refusing bonds issues to pay for prisons. Taxpayer resistance has not deterred the private sector from radically altering the ways correctional facilities are financed and built. Government-issued bonds are being replaced by private lease-purchase arrangements, which are underwritten by such investment firms as E. F. Hutton, Merrill Lynch, Morgan Stanley and Company, Prudential Securities, Smith Barney Shearson, Goldman Sachs, and Shearson Lehman Brothers. The leases allow lots of flexibility and permit governments to make installment purchases of property, which is privately financed and built upon.[8]

Private providers of prisons cite many reasons why they are better-equipped to manage prisons, but the most compelling argument is that they foster competition, which leads to a reduction in costs. Providers also claim that privitization fosters a competitive environment among the employees, who respond by improving cost efficiencies and quality of work. To prove their point that private prisons are better equipped to manufacture savings, proponents of private prisons cite comparative studies that reinforce their argument that private prisons are cheaper to run than publicly managed prisons.[9]

At first glance, the evidence clearly establishes the economic advantages of privatized corrections, but a thorough analysis of the reasons purported for such advantages exposes a number of multi-faceted and subtle factors that contribute to cost savings. For instance, private prisons shy away from managing maximum security prisons because this translates into additional security expenditures for them. Also, private prisons provide medical care for prisoners with minor illnesses and refer those with more serious illnesses to outside doctors, which means the states bear these costs—not the for-profit firm.

A study conducted in Hamilton County, Florida, found that contracting out prison management produced an annual savings of at least 4 to 8 percent, but those conducting the study contend that the savings were more likely in the range of 5 to 15 percent compared to the anticipated cost of direct county management.[10] A study conducted by the University of Florida at Gainesville Center for Studies in Criminology and Law evaluated available data on forty-five privately managed correctional facilities to see if any cost savings were verified. It found ten private facilities that could be compared with a public counterpart. All ten private prisons substantiated cost savings ranging from 10.71 percent to 52.23 percent. While advocates and opponents continue to make their concluding points of view with respect to the advantages and disadvantages of privatized corrections, the jury has deliberated and returned its verdict—privatization saves money, provides quality services, and fulfills a need.[11] However, critics point out the methodological flaws of reports asserting that private prisons save costs and the credibility of the claims given that the agency reeives funding from for-profit prisons.

A report by the General Accounting Office (GAO) contends that five states (California, New Mexico, Tennessee, Texas, and Washington) have observed either cost or quality of service issues connected to public prisons, private prisons, and public prisons that do some degree of private contracting.[12] Three states (California, Tennessee, and Washington) compared costs between public and private facilities.[13] The GAO conducted a review of the four comparisons made between private and public prisons in the three studies, finding that two showed no significant differences in operational costs, one showed a 7 percent difference in favor of the private facility, and the other reported the private facility to be more costly than the public facility.[14] As it concerns cost savings—the issue that proponents of privatization hang their argument on—the GAO found that, with regard to costs, these studies do not offer substantial evidence of savings.[15] However, the GAO's findings are in dispute and this will be discussed in the next section.[16]

Another report authored by pro-privatization organization the Reason Foundation identified twenty-eight studies that analyze cost data to assess the comparative costs of government-managed correctional facilities versus private firms. They found that twenty-two of the studies demonstrated that significant savings were achieved by privatization.[17] However, each of the studies was found to suffer from methodological shortcomings, which lessens the impact of the findings.

Private prisons allege that they are more effective in getting the job done than public prisons, citing the following improvements:

1. Public safety
2. Staff safety
3. Prisoner safety as it relates to victimization from other prisoners
4. Prisoner safety and the effective use of formal disciplinary actions
5. Prisoner safety in respect to medical risks from communicable diseases (such as HIV), contraband, and substance abuse
6. Better work climate, which leads to better-managed prisons
7. More innovative delivery of service, which improves efficiency and, in turn, translates into cost savings

Advocates of private prisons raise questions regarding the fitness of public prisons to manage correctional facilities considering their track record of abuse and mismanagement; however, they neglect to share private prisons' history of abuse. In a *Boston Herald* Op-Ed, the reporter underscores the prevalent assaults on prisoners, overcrowding, drug use, and unhygienic conditions in prisons in the United Kingdom to reinforce claims of abuse.[18] The same report discovered that government officials and prison directors repeatedly "turned a blind eye" to abusive treatment of prisoners.[19] Also noted in this report was the fact that prisoners were being locked in their cells for up to twenty-three hours a day. When allowed to engage in "work, educational and recreational opportunities," the "grossly overcrowded" public prisons manifested "tense" staff-prisoner relations and a "spirit of confrontation."[20]

A review of public prisons in the United States corroborates these finding of abuse in public prisons cited by advocates of privatization.

For those who assert that public prisons are safer, all they have to do is to examine the atmosphere in Massachusetts' public prisons, which are comparable to prisons in the U.K. Many of the prisons in the United States currently operate at or above capacity, and the prisons in Massachusetts are reported to be at 137 percent of capacity[21]—more than 30 percent higher than the national average.[22]

Advocates cite these findings to support their claim that private prisons are better-equipped to provide safety than public prisons. The *Boston Herald* article also found that private prison staff workers displayed more favorable attitudes toward prisoners, and they created a "positive and healthy" atmosphere, which translated into better-managed private prisons.[23] It was also reported that the treatment of prisoners was superior, and the atmosphere was such that creativity was encouraged and unencumbered by bureaucratic restrictions noted in public prisons. Because of this, private providers introduce more innovative ideas, which positively change the prison culture.[24]

A report on private prisons in the United States by the Criminal Justice Institute (CJI) reinforces these findings. The CJI reported that, unlike public prisons, private prisons are not suffering from problems of overcrowding and they are operating at 90.5 percent of capacity.[25] They also report that a higher level of safety is ensured as a result of the lower capacity, and this creates an atmosphere more conducive to good staff-prisoner relations.[26] Advocates of private prisons point out that many public prisons exceed their capacity and are under court order to reduce their prison capacities because of the problems resulting from overcrowding. Proponents of private prisons cite the CJI report to buttress their position on the superiority of private prisons to guarantee public safety. The report by CJI contends that private prisons outperform their public counterparts on many important measures hands down; for instance, private prisons had fewer escapes (70 per 100,000 prisoners) than public prisons (87); fewer incidents of major misconduct (3 incidents versus 7.5 incidents per 10 prisoners) and fewer incidents of general misconduct (3 incidents versus 15 incidents per 10 prisoners); and, most significantly, fewer prisoner deaths due to homicide, suicide, and accidental causes (7 deaths versus 25 deaths per 100,000 prisoners).[27] According to the report, there were also fewer prisoner assaults committed against staff in private prisons.

Advocates of privatization contend that the traditional corrections model based on government-run prisons is antiquated and cannot keep up with the growing needs of public safety. In addition, lawmakers cannot continue to follow the traditional model, which responds to public safety issues by building more prisons, especially in the face of state budget deficits and the public's strong anti-tax sentiment.

According to a report by the Washington Policy Center, the answer to how to pay for needed prison capacity and improve public safety can be found in promoting competition among prisons.[28] In addition, the center has identified four principles that demonstrate how competition can successfully improve quality and ease the budget strain of a core government program:

- Because competition exists in the private sector, they are more efficient, which lowers the cost of performing a service.

- Government has a monopoly and thus fails to operate at higher service levels because it lacks the incentive to innovate and improve service delivery and by improving service delivery, private firms achieve cost savings.

- Government should become more business-like and adopt business practices which are more accurate and comprehensive than traditional government methods.

- If government opened itself to competition like the private sector, it would transform its culture so that a smaller set of core functions could be performed better than ever before, while leaving much of the routine work to contractors.[29]

Moreover, private sector prisons are championed as being innovative because they save money by approaching the management of prisons differently from government. For instance, the claim is supported by the following declaration: the private sector introduces cutting-edge management approaches and enhanced monitoring techniques and fosters a climate replete with innovation. As a result, the advantages private providers have over the public translate into reduced labor costs coupled with reduced tension between the private staff and the prisoners.[30]

Many advocates of private prisons contend that competition, fueled by the profit incentive, ensures that private providers of prisons have a vested interest in public safety, prisoner safety, staff safety, and quality. Advocates further assert that private prisons are superior to public prisons because they trade on the stock exchange, and their performance and reputation affects their future profitability; thus, they have a very high incentive to maintain a safe, secure, and healthy prisoner population.[31]

QUALITY ARGUMENTS

The debate about quality rests on whether the private sector can provide superior programming for prisoners than their public counterparts. The ability to provide quality services for prisoners is key to improving safety. For-profit firms contend that states are unable to provide quality programming for inmates because of budgetary constraints. As a result, public prisons are considered to be less safe than privately managed prisons.

Those who side with privatization declare that the contracting process increases quality for both the government and the private sector because competition is introduced; thus, savings are incurred, which enhances the private agencies' efforts to provide more programmatic activities for prisoners. Furthermore, the debate focuses on other claims of superiority of private prisons—that they can provide faster bed capacity, more accountability, better risk management, greater innovation, new service delivery acquisition, and improved efficiency and flexibility.[32] These factors alone, advocates of privatization declare, demonstrate that their ability to respond promptly to the demand for prison beds creatively and innovatively ensures that they can deliver better quality.

Another reason provided by private prisons is that they have an economic incentive to provide quality in order to avoid prisoner litigation. Any litigation affects their shareholders' profits; as a result, these firms are vigilant regarding how they manage, program, and operate the facilities. In addition, operators of private prisons realize that they can be replaced if they provide inferior service; as a result, the threat of replacement provides a strong incentive to provide quality. The ability to provide quality will affect future contracts; thus, private providers do it better because of the threats of competition and replacement.

Proponents of privatization contend that once public prisons are subject to market pressures introduced by privatization, the competition will certainly produce both greater cost efficiencies and quality improvements in correctional services. They believe the public system is hampered in its quest to produce quality because unions are an impediment to quality. They believe that once that impediment is removed, productivity will increase. Critics contend that unions hamper productivity because they won't allow employees to take on multiple responsibilities, they tend to negotiate too-rigid employment contracts, and many of them take a "just say no" attitude toward reform.

Proponents of prison privatization argue that there is a bevy of information that supports their assertions that private prisons actually improve quality. For instance, the American Correctional Association (ACA), an independent body that accredits correctional agencies found that, of the 5,000 government and privately managed facilities across the United States, only 532 are accredited by the ACA—465 of 4,800 government-managed facilities (10 percent accredited) and 67 of 150 privately managed facilities (44 percent accredited)[33]—thus making the case that privately managed facilities are providing quality and saving money. However, it is alleged that the quality of services delivered by privatization of corrections has been equal or superior to the quality of correctional services delivered by the public sector.

SUMMARY

Scholars have put together chief reasons to either to accept or reject privatization.[34] These motives to accept or reject privatization can be ascribed to the prime desire of many states and local governments to meet the demand for additional prison beds and to reduce prison operational costs.[35] Advocates for more private sector involvement in functions traditionally performed by public agencies support their position with three types of arguments: ideological, economic, and issues regarding efficiency.[36] Proponents for less private involvement in the public sector bolster their view with an additional set of arguments with ethical implications.[37]

Debunking the Efficiency, Effectiveness, and Quality Arguments

CRITIQUE OF THE ECONOMIC/EFFICIENCY ARGUMENT

Reports abound purporting that private prisons are superior when it comes to saving costs. However, recent reports demonstrate that economic and efficiency superiority claims made by private prisons are a myth.[38] For instance, private prisons cite accreditation as a testament to their superiority. They suggest that, because more private prisons are accredited than public prisons, private agencies are able to manage the prisons more efficiently than their public counterparts, which translates into savings. However, an advocacy group against the use of private prisons disputes this fact, contending that research shows that public prisons actually have a higher accreditation rate than private prisons.[39]

The advocacy group also argues that the ACA has never failed any institution pursuing accreditation from them.[40] Their job is to make recommendations only and reevaluate them later to see if they have made the recommended changes.[41] In addition, they point out that "some of the most dangerous and deadly prisons in the country have been ACA accredited; the Tallulah Juvenile Facility in Louisiana is a prime example."[42] In addition, "the ACA is not a governmental agency charged with accrediting prisons and nor is it regulated by an independent outside agency,"[43] which calls into question the legitimacy of ACA accreditation. To top this off, any organization interested in accreditation has to pay ACA to receive accreditation; this clearly undermines the argument by proponents of privatization concerning the superiority of accredited prisons. Implicit in this argument is the idea that for-profit prisons purchase accreditation as oppose to earning accreditation.

Private prisons are often accused of "cherry picking;" that is, they select prisoners that are more manageable, which has favorable cost implications. For instance, companies like CCA opt for younger prisoners who are more likely to be healthier and are less likely to have medical and disciplinary problems. To the private companies that manage facilities, these are ideal prisoners because they are cheaper to maintain. If this reduction of costs were factored in, would private prisons still have a cost advantage over public prisons?

An additional critique of private prisons is that, in a for-profit environment, every dime not spent adds to the company's profits.[44] The introduction of profit not only provides an inducement to hold down costs; it also provides an incentive to increase revenues.[45] This means that increasing a prisoner's sentence can increase the revenue of the for-profit provider. For example, the state-appointed monitor at the Pahokee Youth Development Center in Florida discovered an internal Correctional Services Corporation memo directing staff to hold juveniles beyond their scheduled release dates to increase the company's income by $3,400.[46]

Another example that illustrates the vested interest of private prisons comes from a Tennessee prison under the auspices of CCA. In this prison, some of the CCA guards who were interviewed privately said that they were encouraged to write up prisoners for minor infractions and place them in segregation.[47] The prisoners in segregation not only lose their good time but also have thirty days added to their sentence—a bonus of nearly $1,000 for the company at some prisons.[48] Again, if these costs were factored in the efficiency and economic arguments, for-profit prisons would not be as bold in their claims of superiority.

Proponents of privatization contend that private prisons are able to reduce costs because they are subject to market pressures, while the government's monopoly gives them no incentive to be efficient. However, a review of the private prison landscape suggests that monopolistic conditions exist in the for-profit prison industry as well—private agencies CCA and Wackenhut (now known as the Geo Group Inc.) control over 74 percent of the privately managed beds in the United States.[49] The "big two," as they are called, are often the only companies with enough resources and the infrastructure to go after a contract, while the remaining eight to twelve companies fight over their rejects. The use of speculative prisons, which only CCA and Wackenhut have the capacity to build, has further increased their competitive advantage over the rest of the industry. Speculative prisons often result in a sole-source contract and lead to a competitive advantage for the big two; thus, agencies that own speculative prisons cannot be readily replaced because the company owns the facility.[50] Again, factoring in that competition does not exist in the for-profit industry on the level proponents of prison privatization contend sheds more light on the fact that it is really not known whether private prisons are cheaper to run than public prisons. The debate remains open for discussion.

The for-profit sector claims that competition is an economic advantage and the key to quality. This argument rests on the belief that for-profit operators, knowing they could be replaced if they fail to deliver, have motivation to provide quality service. The assumption is that the system has an abundant supply of competitors; however, this is definitely not the case in the for-profit corrections industry because, as stated, two companies own the majority of the private prisons. This fact alone undercuts this argument. In general, critics of privatization point out that there are a lot of buyers and a very limited number of sellers that differentiate the market in the prison privatization arena.

The market-efficiency argument is also based on the belief that the buyer has adequate information to make a decision; however, we realize that caveat emptor governs the market. Additionally, the lack of public access to the records of for-profit prisons means that the public officials who buy the service, as well as the taxpayers who pay for it, do not have adequate information to make a good decision about prison privatization.[51] Private prisons don't disclose records that discuss the specifics of their contracts, such as who pays for medical costs or who pays for monitoring costs of the prisons. If private prison operators revealed all their costs as opposed to invoking proprietary responses to requests for information, the citizenry could evaluate their claims. However, they are unwilling to disclose information that would allow a comprehensive assessment of who should manage the prison system.

According to Michael Jacobson, Criminal Justice Professor at John Jay College and the University of New York, the costs claim advantages made by private prisons can be disingenuous because they base their per diem figures for prisoners on projections rather than actual expenditures. The private companies that manage prisons compare their projections to existing Department of Correction (DOC) expenditures and leave out the important facts when costing out a new prison. For example, private prisons will hire all new staff at the lowest level of salary and benefits; when new public prisons open, many experienced staff with higher pay rates and benefit packages will transfer into that new facility.[52] The implications of this manner of reporting is deceitful because it makes it look like the private prisons are cheaper to run when in fact they may be more expensive.

The idea that private prisons save money has been undercut by a report from the Office of Program Policy and Analysis and Government Accountability (OPPAGA), an office of the Florida legislature, which found that a contract between the state and CCA for Bay Haven Prison was "structured in such a way to provide excessive payments to the vendor for each additional prisoner in excess of 90% capacity."[53] Although the incident in question is specific to Florida in this case, this represents a long line of strategies employed by private agencies to maximize their profits.

Another example that undermines the claim that private prisons save taxpayers money is found in a report by the American Federation of State, County and Municipal Employees (AFSCME) who report that many of the studies that champion the ability of private prisons to save taxpayer money do not incorporate hidden costs associated with prison privatization.[54] For instance, the study finds that if hidden costs—monitoring, healthcare referrals, and benefit reductions for correction officers—were tallied, privatization would prove to be a more costly to taxpayers than public management. In addition, the report cites prison riots to embellish the above point, contending that, when prisoners riot or cause damage to a facility, most riots are precipitated by substandard conditions caused by the private facility's propensity to cut corners to save money. As a result, the jurisdiction where the riots occurred must assist in restoring control for the private firm.[55] In helping to restore control to the private facility, a cost is incurred by the taxpayer, demonstrating that private prisons are not cheaper to manage when all costs are taken into consideration.

Another piece of information private prisons providers leave out is the fact that they receive sweetheart deals in the form of tax breaks and property rebates from economically depressed communities—especially rural communities in search of jobs. Because of their position in the market, the big two—CCA and Wackenhut—have been able to structure their prison businesses in the form of real-estate investment trusts (REITs), a strategy that allows them to avoid virtually their entire tax burden.[56]

In effect, prisons are actually removing tax dollars from the system when they employ strategies to maximize their bottom line, such as reducing employees' salaries.[57] This is problematic because 60 percent of the costs of incarceration are represented by employee salaries. Because the main means of reducing expenditures for the prison corporations is to reduce those salaries, it stands to reason that this process would have to result in a substantial loss in state and federal income taxes.[58]

The debate still lingers over whether private prisons are better able to manage prisons than public prisons. If an answer is to be found, it may come from scholars who have written extensively on or about privatization. One scholar that fits this category makes the following statement:

> At this stage it is impossible to answer most of the empirical questions about the comparative cost-effectiveness and efficiency of private correctional operations. Though publications on the subject now number in the hundreds, the necessary research has simply not been done, and relevant empirical data remain scarce. Theoretical speculation, anecdotes, and raw statistics abound, but there is as yet little dependable information to tell us whether or how privatization can work, and at what human and financial costs.[59]

Although this article was penned in 1999, this assessment describes the current climate of the private prison industry.

The reports make it clear that the debate is far from over regarding the superiority of private prison management versus public management. These reports also support my claims that broader explanations must be examined to get a sense of the reasons why states really contract. Although there is enough evidence to undermine the arguments that for-profit prisons are cheaper than public prisons, proponents of private prisons continue to argue that they can do it cheaper. However, a report by AFSCME contends that reports that claim for-profit prisons operate more cheaply tend to be flawed for a number of reasons: "First and foremost, they tend to compare 'apples to oranges.'"[60] In other words, many of the comparisons made between public and private prisons are faulty because it is difficult to find comparable facilities to evaluate to determine superiority of services. For instance, "in New Mexico, the one women's prison in the state's correctional department is operated by a for-profit company."[61] According to AFSCME, "finding a comparable publicly operated prison in the state is impossible, as women's prisons are operated quite differently than facilities for men and generally cost more."[62] Another issue in the faulty comparisons claim centers on the fact that government managed prisons mostly house maximum and medium security prisoners and they cost out their expenditures based on housing maximum and medium security prisoners, "while only 2 percent of the prisoner population in for-profit prisons are maximum security prisoners."[63]

The public is misled into believing that private prisons can do it cheaper than their public counterparts because for-profit prisons cite projections of short-term costs as opposed to long-term management costs. This is problematic because many real costs associated with managing a private prison may not manifest themselves for years. Another strategy employed to make it look as if private prisons are cheaper to manage occurs doing the initial bidding of the contract. Private prison operators have been found to specialize in submitting low bids to win contracts to drive out competitors; after they have driven out the competition, they ask for more money because they knew all along that it would take more money to operate the facility than initially anticipated. One case in point is the Monroe County, Florida, prison, in which Wackenhut employed this strategy to secure a contract. After managing the prisons for a short period of time, Wackenhut and Monroe County began to discuss the appropriate staffing level for the prison because county officials were concerned that Wackenhut was managing the prison with an inadequate level of staff.[64] After some discussion, Wackenhut relented and agreed to increase their staffing level, but they solicited an additional $750,000 from the county commissioner to meet the increased staffing level request. The request was denied and, as a result, "the sheriff's office had to take back the jail."[65] Further proof is provided by in a report that shows that Wackenhut was responsible for managing two New Mexico prisons plagued with violence.[66] After continuous problems in these prisons, Wackenhut went back to the Legislative Finance Committee after the initial contract and asked them to increase the state's per diem so they could improve the facilities.[67] Notice that in the cases above, Wackenhut failed to provide the level of services and generate the savings it asserted it could produce during the initial bid.

A note of caution: the excellent data provided by opponents of privatization, such as the large unions that generate reports slamming privatization, can be called into question. These unions are comprised of government employees, and they clearly have a vested interest in seeing privatization fail. The same can be said of the for-profit prison firms; they generate lots of reports that contend that they are superior at saving taxpayers money. Only objective analysis will settle this question that plagues policy makers and taxpayers.

Hidden Costs

Another issue symptomatic of the comparison of public versus private prison management costs is private prisons' omission of "hidden" costs, such as the expense associated with quelling riots and capturing escapees from private prisons. For example, CCA put in place a new reimbursement policy governing what they termed "reasonable expenses" in regards to remuneration for law enforcement agencies searching for CCA escapees.[68] Critics were quick to point out that what is "reasonable, of course, is subject to interpretation."[69] The impetus for this new policy by CCA was a seven-day search conducted by local authorities in Tennessee for two Montana convicts who escaped from the CCA-run West Tennessee Detention Center.[70]

40

The total cost for this search amounted to about $80,000.[71] CCA also had five escapes from their South Central Correctional Center in Tennessee during 1999, compared to none at comparable state-run facilities.[72] These findings suggest that the state incurs a cost for recapturing escapees from private prisons and that these expenses are excluded from the day-to-day running expenditure of private prisons and are not part of the operational account.

Other states with private prisons have had similar problems with escapes, which ended up costing the state money beyond the initial contract. Before states smartened up, many footed the bill for recapturing private prison escapees. For instance, the state of Texas has had for-profit prisons since the mid-1980s, but it was not until more than a decade later that the state passed laws requiring taxpayers to be reimbursed for the mistakes of the private prison providers. To redirect this hidden expense back to the for-profit prisons, Ohio now mandates that for-profit prisons reimburse the state for any assistance it provides in recapturing escapees, a policy that became necessary because of the high number of private prisons escapes and the cost associated with recapturing. For-profit prisons exclude this data when making claims of cost superiority.

There are still other costs that for-profit providers of prisons fail to mention when promulgating their cost superiority: the procurement process costs and indirect costs, such as "legal work and administrative costs, including contract monitoring, and other overhead costs that will not be reduced by privatization."[73] These costs can be significant; failure to include them does not provide a real picture of the expenditure associated with managing a prison. As a result, definitive cost-superiority claims made by private prison providers can and should be called into question. Critics have estimated that failure to calculate procurement and indirect costs misses between 10 to 20 percent of contract costs, which translates into additional costs incurred by the state if they fail to calculate these costs when opening up the management of prisons to bidding.[74]

Another point to consider is that privatization adds a new layer of bureaucracy to government. For example, Florida's Correctional Privatization Commission was created specifically to oversee the privatization of correctional facilities in that state.[75] As other states adopt the practice of creating commissions to regulate private prisons, "the costs of contracting out will continue to mount."[76]

In scrutinizing the contract incentives doled out to for-profit prison firms, it becomes apparent that taxpayers incur costs through the incentives inherent in these contracts. For instance, the contract incentives include minimum prisoner guarantees and caps on health care costs that benefit for-profit firms. The for-profit providers also negotiate contracts that guarantee the company a minimum number of prisoners without thinking about future issues, such as a reduction in the crime rate. These guarantees and incentives can have costly repercussions for government agencies. For example, New Mexico entered into a contract with Wackenhut that required the state to pay for 90 percent occupancy, regardless of actual occupancy at the facility. New Mexico is not alone in this practice. However, after a series of violent incidents at the Wackenhut facility in New Mexico, the state transferred over 100 prisoners to a maximum-security prison a couple of thousand miles away to Virginia. Wackenhut appeared to have systemic problems with violence that jeopardized the safety of the prisoners in the New Mexico facility, which New Mexico felt warranted the transfer of prisoners to Virginia. Regardless of the transfer, Wackenhut insisted that New Mexico still had to pay the negotiated $45 per prisoner per day cost for the empty bed space that resulted from the transfer. An implication of moving the prisons is that New Mexico would have to pay Wackenhut and the state of Virginia for housing the same prisoners, although the prisoners no longer reside in the Wackenhut facility in New Mexico. Moreover, the state of New Mexico "had to pay to transport the prisoners to Virginia and was charged a high fee—$64 per prisoner per day—by Virginia because it required emergency housing. New Mexico could end up paying more than double the original cost to house prisoners."[77]

Still another hidden cost issue for states is the cap on health care costs negotiated by for-profit firms. A report by the American Correctional Association states that "prisoner health care costs increased by 10.24 percent in 1998, and 9.87 percent in 1997."[78] This fact alone makes the contract untenable for states as health care costs continue to rise. Again, it becomes obvious that private prisons may not be cheaper than public prisons when all things are considered equally. An even more perplexing issue is that many states have not learned from other states that have caps on health care costs that favor for-profit firms. For instance, states such as Florida, Nevada, and Tennessee have favorable caps on health care costs for private prison firms that operate in the state. A good example is provided by the state of Florida, which pays medical costs up to $7,500 for the for-profit firms and picks up any costs that exceed this amount. It is glaringly obvious that the caps on health care costs shift the burden of incarceration costs from the for-profit firms to the state. States must consider the following issues before they cap health care costs for for-profit firms:

- The move by states to impose longer sentences
- The spread of communicable diseases
- The increase in prisoners with psychiatric problems, which is one factor expected to increase future health care costs
- The result that taxpayers will increasingly pick up the tab[79]

Cost Incurred to Export Prisoners

When New Mexico exported prisoners from the Wackenhut facility to Virginia, the negative cost consequences for the state were not immediately obvious to the public. New Mexico has lost jobs and future income taxes as a result. The exportation of prisoners impacts the state in other ways as well. For instance, New Mexico will incur costs associated with the loss of grants and federal subsidies tied to the prisoners residing in their state. Prisoners are counted by the U.S. Census as residents of the communities where the prison is located instead of the communities in which they resided before incarceration. By exporting prisoners to another private prison in another state, New Mexico "may lose funding for federal and state programs that base their assistance on population."[80] There also may be long-term implications as a result of exporting prisoners. The recidivism literature posits that the more contact prisoners have with their families, the more likely their reintegration into society will be successful. When prisoners are exported to other states, it makes it difficult for their families to visit or call; all calls made in prison are collect, and prison pay phones can make about $15,000 a day. The networks required to facilitate reintegration are destroyed. Once released, inmates are more likely to return to prison because of the inimical effects of being sent so far away from their families. Finally, taxpayers end up footing the bill to transport prisoners to other jurisdictions outside of the state, which amounts to yet more costs not calculated during the initial prison privatization contract.

Tax Implications

Another issue is the purported property tax contribution private prisons make to the communities. Although often portrayed as a source of tax income to the community, private prisons do not always have an exemplary tax record. For instance, "CCA pulled out of its contract to operate the Cleveland (Ohio) Pre-Release Center because it did not want to pay its share of local taxes."[81] To top this off, "both the city and county had given CCA more than a 50 percent tax abatement from 1995 to 1998, but they still tried to avoid paying taxes."[82] Another example of for-profit prisons' hostility toward paying taxes: "in 1997, CCA paid its property taxes for the Leavenworth (Kansas) Detention Center under protest, arguing that 90 percent of the prison should be classified as residential."[83]

For-profit firms use other strategies to circumvent paying taxes. For instance, Wackenhut agreed in 1994 to "pay Glades County officials about $400,000 a year in property taxes, but later sold the land to a specially created nonprofit entity."[84] The following year, the *Denver Post* reported that "the Florida Correctional Privatization Commission exempted the 750-bed prison from property taxes."[85] The failure to collect property taxes from for-profit prisons is not endemic to Glades County, Florida. A report in the *Tampa Tribune* found that Bay, Columbia, Polk, and Palm Beach counties failed to collect taxes from the for-profit firms CCA and Wackenhut. It should be noted that the practice of taxpayers subsidizing commercial private prisons is not confined to Florida. For instance, "the State of Arizona went so far as to pass a law in 1998 prohibiting the taxation of for-profit firms' income that they generated from incarcerating or detaining prisoners. This was not the strangest move by the state but the law was passed and written to take effect retroactively."[86]

Another interesting strategy to avoid paying taxes transpired when the always-resourceful CCA merged with its Real Estate Investment Trust (REIT), Prison Realty. By merging with its REIT, CCA was able to circumvent the tax code by taking advantage of an ambiguity in the federal tax system that permits REITs to steer clear of taxes at the company level. Although CCA was well within its rights to take advantage of the law, the tax shelter in question was created for legitimate real estate companies. CCA pursued this course of action to avoid paying corporate income taxes on the revenue it generated from operating its private prison. To compound the problem of collecting taxes from for-profit prisons, REITs can also avoid paying taxes at the state level according to a 1999 report presented at the Fourth Annual Privatizing Correctional Facilities Conference in Las Vegas. CCA's plan was simple: whatever revenues were generated should be channeled to its REIT with the sole purpose of shielding their profits from taxes. If the taxes that CCA and other for-profit firms shielded were factored into the cost of managing their prisons, it is highly unlikely that states would consider privatizing their prison systems.

The creativity of for-profit prison companies as it concerns avoiding taxes does not stop at channeling funds to their REITs—they also partner with local economic development agencies to avoid paying taxes. By doing so, for-profit firms are able to get around expensive financing arrangements by getting backdoor taxpayer subsidies for financing through the issuance of tax-exempt bonds. Of course, there are taxpayer costs associated with this type of financing because the development authority might issue securities that pay a higher interest rate than general obligation bonds. Another potential pitfall of this strategy is that the project risk will be shifted to the taxpayer instead of the for-profit firm because if the for-profit firm fails, the government is culpable for the provider's failed performance. For example, in 1988 the Dallas-based Detention Services for-profit prison firm convinced Zavala County, Texas, officials to underwrite a for-profit prison with county bonds to be repaid from their prospective revenues. On top of this, they then contracted with the District of Columbia to house prisoners. However, by December 1990, the

District of Columbia decided to cancel its contract with Detention Services, citing prisoner escapes, excessive fights, and a host of other incidents that called into question the firm's ability to effectively manage the prison. As a result of the District's action, the for-profit prison was left with empty beds and no source of revenue coming into their coffers. With no revenue, Zavala County was forced to make bond payments out of its operating fund, which resulted in the county incurring a deficit and defaulting on the bonds.[87] Again, this is another instance in which the taxpayers end up paying costs that go beyond the original contract.

Liability Costs

Although the state enters into a contract with a for-profit firm, the state is still liable for prisoners held in those prisons. Consider the decision handed down by a state judge in Montana in 1999 concerning the state corrections department claim that they were not responsible for prisoners held in for-profit prisons. The judge ruled that the state corrections department was indeed culpable.[88] States that contract with private prison providers are also misled by for-profit firms who claim that they will fully cover the state from liability. Although this assurance by the for-profit prison is a smart concession that the state should require of them, the state is still liable because this guarantee can be difficult to enforce. For example, CCA contracted with the District of Columbia for $182 million to house prisoners in its Youngstown, Ohio, facility, and the District officials were told by CCA officials that the facility was fully indemnified. However, it was revealed that the CCA facility was not indemnified, and the District of Columbia's only recourse was to sue CCA to force their compliance with the contract because CCA was unwilling to fulfill its promise. The lawsuit initiated by the District of Columbia alleged that CCA refused to indemnify the Youngstown facility as promised, and they failed to obtain the requisite insurance policy naming the District as insured.[89]

Research reveals that evidence is mounting against for-profit firms' ability to secure sufficient liability insurance. For instance, the for-profit firm Cornell Corrections Inc. declared in its November 18, 1999, SEC filing that "we are unable to secure insurance for some unique business risks including riot and civil commotion or the acts of an escaped offender."[90] In another early example, CCA entered into a contract with Hamilton County, Tennessee, and the contract stipulated that CCA should indemnify the facility for $25 million in insurance to protect the county from liability. However, the county found out that CCA did not have this amount after they consummated the contract. On top of this revelation, the *Phoenix Gazette* reports that the County found out that not only did CCA fail to indemnify the facility as promised, but they could not even get anyone to underwrite the policy.[91]

Other factors that erode for-profit firms' claim that they are more cost-effective than the public sector is the fact that employees of private prisons do not have the same protection as employees of public prisons. Government officials at all levels are protected from being sued for performing their job as long as they do not infringe upon "clearly established rights that a reasonable person should have known." "In *Richardson v. McKnight*, the Supreme Court in a 5–4 opinion delivered by Justice Stephen G. Breyer held that prison guards employed by a private firm are not entitled to qualified immunity from a lawsuit by prisoners charging a section 1983 violation. Emphasizing that a private firm was systematically organized to manage the prison,"[92] Justice Breyer wrote that, "[o]ur examination of history and purpose...reveals nothing special enough about the job or about its organizational structure that would warrant providing these private prison guards with governmental immunity."[93] After further review, the cost claims made by advocates of for-profit prison firms may not hold up to scrutiny in light of the fact that indemnification agreements between jurisdictions and for-profit prison vendors may not be enforceable, thus shifting the liability for the provision of public services back to the government agency.

For-profit firms provide ample evidence to support their claims of cost reductions, but enough evidence has been provided here to question those claims. Until studies are conducted that calculate all possible costs associated with managing a prison, the evidence to support superiority claims will remain anecdotal. The fact that there are no current methodologically sound studies also reinforces the point that it is difficult to compare private and public prisons. Several issues remain that prohibit cost comparisons between public and private prisons. Until these costs issues are ironed out, the likelihood of seeing methodologically sound costs comparisons between public and private prisons is still far off.

CRITIQUE OF THE EFFECTIVENESS ARGUMENT

For-profit firms contend that they are more effective at management than public prisons, especially in the areas of ensuring the safety of the public, staff, and prisoners. One of the requirements necessary to ensuring prisoner and staff safety is making sure that the facility is adequately staffed; however, because of their profit-maximizing behavior, private prisons are habitually understaffed. For example, in North Carolina, a state monitor found that the for-profit firm U.S. Corrections Corporation frequently allowed sixty-eight correctional officers to supervise 528 prisoners; the state prisons used 141 officers to supervise the same number of prisoners.[94] Another example that reinforces the fact that private prisons participate in profit-maximizing strategies that undermine the safety of the facility was shared with the Tennessee legislative panel in October 1997 by a state monitor who monitors for-profit firms for the Virginia Department of Corrections. According to *The Nation*, the monitor found that for-profit firm officials in Texas leave positions in their facility vacant longer than they should as a way to mitigate the impact low reimbursement rates have on their bottom line.[95] By leaving positions vacant longer than they should be, for-profit firms undermine their own arguments that they are safer than public prisons by creating undue stress on their correctional officers, who are understaffed and underpaid. This creates a combustible environment for the prisoners and the staff, two of the main entities that the for-profit firms allegedly make safer because they are—in their own words—more effective at managing prisons.

For-profit firms also maximize profits by paying lower wages to their employees and scrapping the guaranteed pensions systems that the states normally have for their employees and replacing them with cheaper, riskier stock-ownership/option plans. By paying less money and exchanging benefits for cheap stock options, private prisons ensure that they will hire a less-qualified correctional officer, which has negative consequences for their ability to be more effective and to provide higher quality service. Their practice of paying less money and watering down benefits is very degrading to their workforce and has been linked to higher levels of turnover in for-profit prisons. As a byproduct, for-profit firms end up with a less experienced and undertrained prison staff. Furthermore, "the existence of such under-qualified employees, when coupled with insufficient staffing levels, adversely impacts correctional service quality and prison safety."[96]

For example, in 1995 in Elizabeth, New Jersey, at the privately operated Immigration and Naturalization Service (INS) detention center for illegal aliens, prisoners were abused by underpaid, inade-quately trained guards who were under contract with the for-profit firm Esmor Correctional Services (now known as Correctional Services Corporation). Guards at this facility had to endure a riot that involved 300 prisoners. Twenty illegal immigrants were injured dur-ing the riot. In addition, the detainees seized control of the building to voice their opposition to being mistreated; they demolished the interior of the building and held two guards hostage for five hours before police managed to quell the riot. The INS launched an inves-tigation to determine the reasons for the riot, and their investigation found that Esmor officials failed to exercise control over their guards, who were found to be improperly trained or had not been fully inves-tigated before being hired by Esmor. During the riots, it was revealed that Esmor prison guards were paid only $8.00 an hour, or $16,640 a year. After reviewing the *Corrections Yearbook*, it is obvious that this is well below the normal pay for correctional officers; in the same year of the riot, entry-level correctional officers in New Jersey earned $31,805 per year[97]—almost double the earnings of the Esmor guards. Coupled with low pay, poor benefits, high turnover, and low morale, private prisons have yet to prove that they are more effective in man-aging prisons.

A more recent example of underpaid and undertrained staff at a private prison is reported in the *Tulsa World*. The paper reports that the for-profit firm Avalon Correctional Services investigated the cir-cumstances around a prisoner escaping from their Tulsa facility on a Friday but was not noticed missing by officials until Saturday[98] In several newspaper articles summarized by the Private Corrections

Institute Inc., there are cases of prisoner abuse, public safety missteps, high turnover, and management breakdown—all in areas where private prison providers claim they have an advantage over public prisons. As a matter of fact, the Associated Press reports in the last summary noted that the turnover rate at the Whiteville Correction Facility in Tennessee was 86.1 percent. For more articles that undermine the effectiveness argument made by private prisons, please see the Web site of the Florida Police Benevolent Association Inc. (http://www.flpba.org).

CRITIQUE OF THE QUALITY ARGUMENT

For-profit providers claim that they provide superior programming for prisoners. They have even boasted that, because of their superior programming, they are more successful at reducing recidivism.[99] This report, *A Comparative Recidivism Analysis of Releasees From Private and Public Prisons in Florida*, was called into question by Gilbert Geis, Alan Mobley, and David Shichor, who pointed out that the report, which claimed that private prisons are better at reducing recidivism, should be called into question because of one author's conflict of interest—the principal author, Charles Thomas, clearly stood to gain from this report.[100]

The report of Geis, Mobley, and Shichor also illustrates how involved Thomas was in the for-profit firms. For instance, it was discovered that, at the time of this report, he was the director of the Private Corrections Project, which was housed within the Center for Studies in Criminology at the University of Florida. Critics argue that, by not disclosing that the Private Corrections Project was primarily industry-funded (estimated to be around $400,000) by for-profit prison firms, Thomas was unethical in promoting this report without disclosing his conflict of interest. Additionally, by not mentioning that he received a $25,000 summer stipend from those firms, his authority to speak on private prisons claims of superiority in the area of quality is clearly challengeable.[101] In addition, Thomas became a member of the Board of Trustees "of the CCA-offshoot Prison Realty Trust—a REIT."[102] As a board member of CCA's REIT, Thomas received $12,000 a year, plus $1,000 for each board meeting and $500 for each meeting of subcommittees at the time his report was released.[103] These facts are not the most egregious when one takes into consideration that the report makes reference to an October 18, 1998, report by the Securities and Exchange Commission, which showed that the principal received a $3 million fee for facilitating the merger between CCA and Prison Realty Trust.[104] Finally, Geis and colleagues found that the principal owned 30,000 shares of the Realty Trust stock, which at the time of the report was worth $600,000.[105]

The facts found in the report by Geis, Mobley, and Shichor about *A Comparative Recidivism Analysis* reveals one of the main reasons why there is no definitive research available that truly assesses which entity is best suited to handle the management of prisons. Just about all reports for prison privatization are authored by those with a vested interest in privatization, and almost all reports that are against privatization are just as self-interested. The challenge is to generate more independent nonpartisan reports that assess which entity is better equipped to manage prisons—assuming that a neutral report can be written.

Another issue with implications for recidivism, reported in various studies, audits, and newspapers, is that for-profit firms do not provide the kind of services deemed necessary to reintegrate prisoners into society. For instance, a comparative analysis of prisons managed by CCA versus Minnesota public prisons found that the prisons in Minnesota were more likely to have instructors that were properly licensed and credentialed than the private prisons. Another finding of this study was that prisoners in public prisons were accorded an opportunity to attend full time educational and vocational classes. Public prisons were also more likely to have full time intensive chemical dependency treatment programs than their private counterparts, who failed for nearly two years to provide a full time treatment program required by the service contract.[106]

The issue of accountability looms large in the quality debate because for-profit firms are not subject to the open meetings and open records requirements of their government counterparts. As a result, it is difficult for the public to determine if the for-profit firm is committed to quality or spending the public's tax dollars judiciously. Even as abuse cases pile up or when the for-profit firm fails to meet the obligations of the contract because of poor performance, the private firms still may not be required to disclose information to public officials or the press. The Freedom of Information Act (FOIA) is circumvented by for-profit firm's proprietary claims that releasing data compromises their competitive advantage. A case in point is the Department of Corrections in Kentucky, which conducted an investigation and discovered cases of inappropriate use of canteen profits by the U.S. Corrections Corporation.[107] Word leaked to the press, but when the press attempted to follow up on this story, it could not get U.S. Corrections Corporation to release any financial information because Kentucky law exempts for-profit prison companies from disclosing financial records to the public. Even without the protection of the law, it is still next to impossible to get records from private prison operators. Not releasing financial records to the public makes it that much harder to assess the viability of for-profit firm's claims that they are better at providing quality.

Under normal circumstances, the proprietary claim made by for-profit prison firms seems reasonable; however, the need for public disclosure trumps the right to proprietary issues when the government transfers the right to punish to an entity that benefits from punishment; thus, all efforts at transparency should be encouraged when the transfer is made, and that means that proprietary claims should not be applicable to corrections. When prisoners escape from a private facility, the public and its representatives should be provided the details surrounding the escape because public safety is jeopardized. However, five prisoners escaped from the CCA facility in Youngstown, Ohio, in 1998, and CCA was unwilling to provide answer to the legislative advisory group tasked with investigating the incident.[108] In addition, the legislative hearings held to investigate the escape at the Youngstown Facility were met by CCA's in-house attorney instead of the facility's warden. Normal protocol in a state prison requires the warden to answer any questions associated with an investigation of that facility. Not only did CCA not send the warden to the hearing, but after the escape, they also denied access to the facility to the Ohio Correctional Institution Inspection Committee, which consists of legislators tasked with inspecting private prisons and state prisons.[109]

In the past, organizations have had to sue for-profit firms to acquire proprietary information that should be subject to FOIA. For instance, the ACLU sued Wackenhut to obtain information about prisoner abuse and sexual harassment of prisoners in one of their Florida facilities. Their suit came on the heels of a suit by *The Ledger*, a Lakeland, Florida, newspaper. The newspaper won its suit against Prison Health Services Inc., a for-profit prison health care provider.[110] Although there has been some success litigating requests for private prison records, as these for-profit firms balance sheets continue to surge past the billion dollar revenue mark, it will become more difficult for the public to battle these for-profit prison conglomerates.

Audits are one way that states have tried to verify the purported gains achieved by privatization in the area of quality and to circumvent the proprietary strategies used by for-profit firms. Based on a set of audits in 1999, for-profit firms did not fare well on these audits. For example, during a routine audit of a CCA facility in Georgia, the Georgia Department of Corrections found that the health care services CCA provided to prisoners was substandard. The audit somewhat substantiated that for-profit firms are often understaffed because the audit revealed that CCA kept unmanned posts and lacked supervision over tools that prisoners could convert to weapons.[111] A subsequent audit as reported by *The Florida Times Union* in 1999 was conducted later in the year on the same facilities and found that CCA was "still not complying with its multimillion-dollar contract."[112] CCA is not alone in its inability to meet the service needs of its prisoners as revealed by audits. There have been other for-profit firms who have had negative findings on audits conducted by the government. For instance, the *Albuquerque Journal* reported the findings of an interior audit conducted on a Wackenhut facility in New Mexico in 1999. The audit uncovered various deficiencies, such as prisoner classification problems and discipline problems.[113]

Moreover, another way to assess the quality claims made by for-profit firms is to look at how many contracts have been terminated and whether the for-profit firms have complied with the contracts or have failed to fulfill the services outlined in the contract by the government agencies.[114] A good source of information about the number of for-profit prison contracts terminated is the AFSCME Web site (http://www.afscme.org), which compiles and summarizes several reports on contract terminations and puts forward the reports on contract terminations to question the argument that for-profit firms superiority claims in the area of quality.

Most of the cases AFSCME summarizes on their Web site happened about five years ago and are somewhat dated; however, the 1990s saw correctional privatizations grow at an alarming rate, and during the late 1990s privatization reached its peaked and leveled off. In reexamining prison privatization in the 1990s, many of the problems for-profit firms encountered during the imprisonment binge could have been adverted if the for-profit providers would not have viewed efficiency, effectiveness, and quality as a means to more profits. Because they viewed efficiency, effectiveness, and quality as routes to monetary gain, they pursued strategies to reduce costs, which led to an erosion of those very areas in which they claimed they could outperform the public. The strategy also made their position that they are better equipped to manage prisons untenable. By viewing efficiency, effectiveness, and quality only in monetary terms, for-profit providers lost track of the real issues that lead to an improved bottom line: prisoner care; safety for prisoners, staff, and the public; and a quality environment for prisoners and staff.

On the other hand, states are culpable for many of the failings of the for-profit providers during the early stages of the prison privatization binge, which eventually lead to increased correctional costs for them. States failed because they designed poor contracts devoid of performance incentives for for-profit prison providers. The contracts initially neglected to address who pays for recovering escapees, indemnification, and monitoring costs; therefore, these costs ended up being the state's responsibility. Both for-profit providers and governments have learned from their early mistakes, and they both do a better job at managing the relationship. This is not to suggest that for-profit prisons have stopped pursuing strategies that improve their bottom line; however, it does suggest that they have become smarter at managing the contracts that have been entrusted to them by the state. In addition, they have gained powerful allies in rural communities, and the legislators of those communities have a vested interest in seeing them excel; thus, the scrutiny from the communities that rely on their largesse may be the reason why the public does not hear as much about their failings as it did during the 1990s.

Does Competition Exist in the For-Profit Prison Environment?

The most vociferous claim made by for-profit providers concerning their quality advantage over the public prisons system is that competition exists in the for-profit prison sector as opposed to the government sector. The chief reason why competition is important in the for-profit environment is that failure to provide quality guarantees that a for-profit firm can be replaced by a competitor. Proponents of privatization contend that, unlike the government, which has a monopoly, for-profit firms have an incentive to provide quality. An implicit assumption in their argument is that competition exists in the for-profit prison environment. However, this is not the case in this industry.[115] The for-profit prison market is "characterized by many buyers (in this case the jurisdictions) and a very limited number of sellers."[116]

It is also reported that CCA and Wackenhut "control over 74 percent of the privately managed beds in the United States."[117] In reviewing all the for-profit firms' annual reports, revenues for CCA and Wackenhut far exceed the other for-profit firms, which accords them an advantage in pursuing contracts because of their resources. Because two companies own 74 percent of the for-profit prisons, most would opine that competition does not exist, making the competition argument a theoretical rather than practical one.

Proponents of privatization have been very persuasive in arguing that they provide better quality than government-managed prisons, but opponents of privatization have argued effectively that this is not the case. Based on the data reviewed, both parties demonstrate that in some areas private prisons are more effective in delivering correctional services and in other areas public prisons are more effective. As a result of the inconclusiveness of their findings, chapter three looks at broader issues that may have influenced the states' decision to seek prison privatization.

This chapter has documented the lack of definitive evidence regarding whether the public or private sector is better equipped to manage prisons. There is support on both sides of the aisle for their claims of superiority, but there is equal support for public prisons. However, the chapter does reinforce my point that broader explanations should be examined to round out the discussion on why states privatize their prisons. Examining broader explanations versus the piecemeal or case-by-case approach that normally shapes the prison privatization debate is essential. In addition, considering the decision to privatize prisons across the United States is an important piece of the puzzle. Despite the efforts to privatize, no other studies have examined the decision to privatize using U.S. data.

Chapter Three

A Framework for Prison Privatization

Introduction

As discussed in chapter two, the standard explanations of efficiency, effectiveness, and quality lead to a piecemeal or micro perspective of prison privatization. This perspective provided by proponents of prison privatization is too narrow to explain what actually happens when the state considers privatizing its prisons. The rebuttals by opponents of privatization are just as inadequate in explaining why states should maintain control of prisons. As a result, standard arguments are inconclusive in determining whether prisoners and taxpayers are better served when prisons are managed by the public sector versus the private sector. Each party has been able to explain their position just as effectively and, because of their skill in explaining their positions, the public is still not sure which entity is better equipped to manage prisons. What is obvious is that the parties involved in the debate are very partisan concerning their position, and this impacts their ability to look at the debate objectively. As a result, the reports generated either for or against privatization are subjective on both sides of the aisle. This lack of objectivity on the part of both parties and the inability to find assessments of cost claims that meet methodological rigor requires that the claims of superiority be further explored in-depth to provide a more objective view. To look at anything empirically is to examine it based on observation or experience;[1] the aim of looking at the data empirically is to help "express a degree of confidence that a relationship we detect is more than a chance occurrence in the one sample that we are able to observe."[2]

The standard explanations of efficiency, effectiveness, and quality all have economic underpinnings for the state. But they are too narrow because they limit their debate to costs and savings to the state and fail to look at other reasons that drive the debate, such as political culture, campaign financing, and economic development. As a result, very little research addresses broader explanations for why states privatize their prisons. While scanning the literature for issues other than the standard explanations that drove the decision to privatize, three themes emerged: economic, ideological, and political. I tested each of the explanations in the respective themes across the fifty states using a statistical program that determines the relationship between the dependent variable (the variable being influenced) and independent variables (the variable that influences the dependent variable). In this study, the decision to privatize was the dependent variable, and I tested twelve independent variables to determine their influence in explaining each state's privatization decision. If the independent variables were significant, it meant that there was a relationship between the independent variables and the dependent variable. In other words, in this analysis, the significant variable predicts that the state's decision to privatize may have been influenced by this variable.

The economic issues at the state level are better suited to explain the decision to privatize than the standard explanations because state-level issues capture the nuisances involved in the policy-making process. For instance, although attempts were made to test the standard explanations, they all fell short because of methodological defects. They considered costs and quality arguments as the only reasons to privatize; they did not compare similar facilities; and they failed to rule out other explanations as to why states' sought prison privatization. The economic issues—corrections expenditures, per capita income, tax capacity, and tax effort—are better barometers to test because they capture the nuisances involved in decision-making, such as the lobbying involved in appropriating money to an agency, the economic health of the state, and the states' priorities. Testing the economic issues injected objectivity into the debate. Additionally, the variables were tested to demonstrate that the decision to privatize is not restricted to saving money. The military base closure saga demonstrates that politics trumps economic prudence. For instance, the commission to evaluate military base closure recommended to the Department of Defense (DOD) that several military bases needed to be closed or realigned. The DOD made these recommendations known to Congress, but senators and congresspeople from the districts targeted for closure circumvented the DOD's recommendations. Based on this example, it is apparent that decision-making is more complex than what is described in the standard explanations. A broader perspective of the debate needs to be pursued for the public to fully understand the dynamics of this phenomenon of state prison privatization. This chapter examines this debate from that broadened perspective.

The ideological variables focus on the role politics plays in influencing the decision to privatize. The variables are legislative control, the governors' party, political ideology, the ideological orientation of the citizens of the state, and state ideology. Again, by examining the debate from a broader perspective, it becomes apparent that the standard reason for why states seek privatization is inadequate. By focusing only on costs as the rationale for privatization, we miss the influence-peddling that takes place during the decision-making process to award a prison to a for-profit firm. It also fails to examine how campaign contributions to legislators and governors from for-profit firms influence privatization decisions. Additionally, confining the debate to costs and quality discussions does not just miss out on the influence of the "get tough on crime" and "war on drugs" campaigns initiated on minority communities via ALEC's Criminal Justice Task Force Committee, an organization funded by private prisons and an organization comprised of many state legislators. It also fails to recognize that conservatives orchestrated these campaigns to foster privatization of prisons for the sake of securing profits for a few well-connected politicians.

A point of clarification is in order, regarding the ideological issues, to distinguish between the way political culture and ideology is discussed regarding their impact on the privatization decision. In this discussion, political culture is employed to examine the citizen ideology of the state, which is a separate issue from the ideology of the governor or the legislature.

Another point that needs to be clarified is that the governor's party can be a political variable, but it also is an ideological variable. The ideological attributes of the variable are more important in explaining the relationship between the existence of private prisons and the ideology of the governor's party as opposed to whether or not the governor's party identified itself as Democratic or Republican. Ideology mattered more than party, and although the distinction is small, it is very important in the decision processes of states as they considered privatizing their prisons.

Finally, the political variables—crime rate, neighboring states, political culture, and prison capacity—demonstrate the intersection of economics and politics in the decision to privatize. Again, a broader explanation is sought to shed light on the reasons states sought privatization of their prisons. For example, the costs and quality discussion misses the point made by critics, who point out that private agencies will lobby for stiffer penalties like mandatory sentencing because when prisons are privatized, profits become the motivating factor for those private agencies that manage prisons.[3] The argument neglects the point that, when private agencies become a part of the equation, this changes the relationship and creates a subgovernmental change; that is, the system of closed networks is now open to potential conflicts of interest because profits are now the most significant feature as a stake and goal with the criminal justice subgovernment.[4] If the prison is public, politicians are not lobbied by for-profit firms who can make campaign contributions to influence policy, nor do they have the incentive to do so. Clearly, focusing only on costs and quality issues does a disservice to the public, who would more than likely look at the privatization of prisons differently if they were aware of the inherent conflict of interest private prisons present.

Another point of clarification is in order here, and it concerns the crime rate as a political variable. It is evident that the politicalization of the crime rate by politicians campaigning on the "get tough on crime" platform required that the variable be examined from a political perspective. In addition, although the crime rate was declining in many states, the "get tough on crime" platform created fear and led to support of laws such as mandatory sentencing and "three-strikes-and-you're-out." It should be noted that many of the laws were sponsored by ALEC. As a result of the political manipulation of the crime rate and the cozy relationship between legislators and for-profit firms, the crime rate became a political variable instead of a criminal problem.

The relationship between legislators, ALEC, and for-profit firms and the politicalization of crime are the unresolved issues and unanswered arguments in the debate regarding the efficacy of allowing prisons to be privately managed. To me, these are the real issues that trump the standard explanations addressed in chapter two, and they will be discussed here. Having tipped my hand regarding the real issues surrounding state prison privatization, a discussion on the broader explanations are addressed in this chapter.

Economic Explanations

The issues of overcrowded prisons, increased correctional costs, and the states' inability to deal with the increasing crime rate provided justification for states to seek prison privatization. Assessing a state's ability to respond to these issues requires a review of the state's environment during the prison privatization movement. In the 1990s, state governments underwent tremendous changes[5] attributed to President Reagan's New Federalism, which transferred more program responsibilities to the states through new unfunded federal mandates, leading to large increases in required state revenues.[6] Coupled with the economic recessions of 1981–1983 and 1991–1992, many state budgets ended up in the red.[7] State governments reacted by cutting services, enacting lotteries, and even raising taxes, despite the tax revolt of the late 1970s.[8] This tax revolt was the public's way of expressing to policy makers that taxes were reaching unacceptably high levels in many states. Additionally, as a result of the intense budget pressures felt by states and the ideology of the Reagan

Revolution, state government leaders became more amenable to the private sector for answers through contracting out, private-public partnerships, and management techniques such as strategic planning and Total Quality Management.[9]

Along with the public's intolerance of tax hikes and the increasing fiscal pressures and corrections expenditures that states were experiencing, policy makers believed that they had very few options other than seeking privatization. As agencies began to compete for funding in fiscally strapped states, the amount being spent on corrections began to disturb policy makers.[10] Many legislators attempted to curb correctional spending when the crime rates began to decline from their peak levels of the late 1980s and early 1990s, but their efforts were thwarted by the persistent demands for harsher sentencing, reductions in good-time credits required by truth-in-sentencing statutes, and stricter handling of parole violators, which pushed state prison populations to even higher levels.[11] In 1996, the number of prisoners in state and federal facilities increased another 5 percent, while the reported violent crime rate declined nationwide by 8 percent.[12]

Twenty years ago, prison cost represented only 1 percent to 2 percent of most state budgets, but now they are in the range of 8 percent to 10 percent and for the past five years have represented the fastest-growing budget category of the fifteen budget items.[13]

Another reason why the increase spending on corrections was problematic for legislators is captured here:

> Increasing expenditures on building and operating additional state prisons is troublesome to state officials for a number of reasons. First, there are many other competing demands for scarce state budget dollars, and only a small portion of the budget can be shifted from one category to another. Increasing prison expenditures usually comes at the expense of higher education, funding for environmental projects, and other such discretionary budget categories. Second, prison construction and operating costs are not seen as adding to a state's capital infrastructure in the way that reductions in class size or increases in technology and training are. Nobody expects ex-prisoners to

make much of a contribution to a state's economy. The whole point is to reduce the drag they exert on it. Finally, there is the issue of the permanence of prison facilities. Just about every prison facility ever opened in this country is still in operation. Prisons seem to last forever. There is a genuine concern among some policy makers that, even as the current crime wave recedes, sentencing and parole release decisions will be changed to ensure that all available prison facilities continue to remain full.[14]

To reinforce the above point, consider the following: the United States has surpassed all countries in the number of people it incarcerates. That number has reached more than two million people. As a result of its expanding prison population, the United States now has to "spend more money on corrections than on the Department of Education, Environmental Protection Agency and Foreign Aid (except the Iraqi package)."[15] Spending on corrections has also outpaced spending on Medicare and Medicaid.[16] The next point brings the debate into focus even more when you consider the fact that state-level spending on corrections increased 95 percent in the 1980s but decreased by 6 percent for higher education during this period.[17] This trend continued into the 1990s because the U.S. appropriated more money toward building prisons ($2.6 billion) than building classrooms ($2.5 billion).[18]

Another culprit that drove state spending on corrections was the 1995 Crime Bill. It forced legislators to appropriate more money for corrections by making $10 billion in prison construction funds available to the states. However, a state had to spend $3 to $5 million of its own money, which meant that they possibly had to redirect money away from education, infrastructure, or health care as an unfortunate side-effect.

The last fifteen years has also brought an increase in state spending on corrections by "350 percent—compared to 250 percent growth for spending on public welfare and 140 percent growth for spending on education."[19] In spite of all this spending, "today many state and federal prisons are holding over 20 percent more prisoners than their capacity, and a great number of facilities—even entire state and county systems—are under court order to limit or reduce their prisoner population."[20]

Scholars attempt to put the discussion in perspective when they ask what all these developments mean for state policy makers as they consider corrections issues and budgets.[21] Critics believe that, in order to answer this question, it is fruitful to review what drives corrections spending. The two biggest factors are the number of prisoners and the length of incarceration.[22] This is an important observation and it parallels the point critics make in regards to the belief that states will lobby for stiffer sentences and laws like mandatory sentencing. If the number of prisoners and length of stay are the two main factors that drive correctional spending, it follows that for-profit firms benefit from laws that incapacitate prisoners for longer periods of time and they ensnare more prisoners than normal. The "war on drugs" and the "get tough on crime" campaigns are primary examples of initiatives that meet those criteria. These campaigns have wreaked havoc on state budgets and have been godsends for the for-profit firms. In addition, scholars' observations are supported when you consider the fact that the number of state prisoners has more than doubled in a decade, growing from 500,564 prisoners in 1986 to almost 1.1 million by the end of 1996.

Furthermore, census figures also show that corrections costs, though a relatively small part of overall state spending, have grown steadily over the past twenty-five years.[23] This assessment is in line with other evaluations of the steady growth of correction expenditures. Societal pressures, driven in part by the media and fueled by politicians, have led to a crack down on crime through mandatory and longer sentences, which have led to burgeoning prison populations and the need for new prison construction.

Based on the ever-expanding correctional costs, one would assume that correctional expenditures played a role in why states sought prison privatization, especially in light of the fact that, in fiscal year 2001, correctional authorities spent $38.2 billion to maintain the nation's state correctional systems, including $29.5 billion specifically for adult prisons.[24] This represented about 77 percent of state correctional costs in the 2001 fiscal year. That same year, state correctional expenditures increased by 145 percent. [25]

Armed with these facts, there should have been a clear indication that correctional expenditures influenced the decision to privatize; however, when tested, there was no observed association between the amount spent on corrections and the decision by states to privatize. The finding was unexpected given the growth of correctional expenditures and the concern expressed by legislatures about growing correctional expenditures.

Correctional spending is at the heart of for-profits firms' argument of cost reduction. This is an enticing claim for policy makers given the amount that is being spent on corrections. However, the test conducted in this study does not support the fact that correctional spending drove the states decision to privatize. The argument regarding costs does not hold in the standard explanations for why states sought prison privatization nor does it hold when testing costs empirically. There must be other reasons why states privatize. Concern over growing correctional costs could be an explanation for why states sought privatization, and lobbying by for-profit firms may be another.

PER CAPITA INCOME

Although per capita income was not one of the reasons provided for why states sought prison privatization, it was a natural variable to examine because of what it reveals about the state's economic well-being. A lot can be learned about a state by looking at its per capita personal income.[26] For instance, the net effect of states' natural resources, national and international economic trends, and the flow of federal funds are reflected in state wealth, usually measured by per capita personal income.[27] Growth in a state's per capita income also serves as a good indicator of the state's economic viability. A review of the census substantiates the fact that there are significant disparities in income between states and between regions. Southern states are likely to be poorer than northeastern states; thus it would follow that southern states would be more amenable to privatization because of their limited resources to respond to increasing correctional costs. However, poverty is not confined to the South; there are many rural communities across the United States that are very poor and also likely to be amenable to privatization initiatives based on their below-average per capita income and limited resources.

A study by the University of Georgia's Carl Vinson Institute of Government corroborates the fact that poverty is concentrated in the southeastern part of the country. They find that poverty has existed within that region "over three census periods (1980, 1990, and 2000) and it is the poorest of all regions of the country."[28] The Southeast also lags behind in several sociodemographic areas, which are indications of the region's economic well-being: education, health, employment, and housing.[29] Lagging behind in these areas further aggravates the cycle of poverty that has been so persistent in this part of the country.

Like the southeastern region, rural communities across the United States suffer the same persistent problems, which leave them vulnerable and, in the end, make them more amenable to options such as privatization. This is seen as an option to help meet public demand for services they are not able to pay for otherwise because of low per capita incomes and sociodemographic problems. However, being poor does not necessarily mean that those states will pursue privatization; however, it does mean that they are more likely to consider alternative means such as privatization to address fiscal concerns.

When the per capita income variable was tested to see if a relationship existed between those states with low per capita income and prison privatization, a relationship was found to exist. This may explain why many of the private prisons are concentrated in the South. This finding helps support the contention of proponents of privatization that lobbying and politics is not involved in the decision to privatize. However, it is not that simple, especially when we consider that Alaska and Hawaii, which have some of the highest per capita incomes in the United States, continue to send prisoners to private prisons out of state even though they have the resources to build their own prisons and house their own prisoners. Critics assert that citizens in both states voted against private prisons because of safety concerns. They also contend that the exportation of prisoners by Alaska and Hawaii to other states demonstrates the lengths that private prisons will go to secure prisoners. Why else might two of the richest states send prisoners out of state if they could build their own prisons? The answer, critics believe, lies in the connectedness of the for-profit providers and their ability to lobby legislators and governors; many owners of for-profit firms are former high ranking government officials. Detractors of privatization also rebut the argument that low per capita income predicts the state's decision to pursue prison privatization by pointing to the fact that New Jersey, one of the wealthiest states in the northeast, has a private prison and sends inmates to other states. However, New Jersey does not have a well-managed budget, and recent reports state that the New Jersey budget is overdrawn by $4 billion. Finally, opponents of privatization contend that lobbying and politics drives the decision to privatize, not the states fiscal condition.

TAX CAPACITY

Another variable that may yield valuable information about state privatization is the states' tax/fiscal capacity, one that gauges the fiscal health of the state. Per capita income has normally been the measure the federal government has used as an indicator of states' relative fiscal well-being.[30] However, the U.S. Advisory Commission on Intergovernmental Relations (ACIR) has proposed that fiscal capacity be measured by a method it has developed, the Representative Tax System (RTS), suggesting that RTS is a better measure of the economic well-being of a state. If the RTS is better, then the findings concerning per capita income are open to debate because the measure may not be a good predictor of a state's privatization decision. Moreover, the RTS defines the tax (or fiscal) capacity of a state and its local governments as the amount of revenue it would raise if it applied a set of national uniform tax rates. The tax rates used for the calculation are representative in the sense that they are the national average rate for each tax base.[31]

An important point about tax capacity is that it can be defined as the "capability of a governmental entity to finance its public services."[32] Both tax capacity and tax effort are frequently measured with instruments developed by the ACIR. Numerous studies of state policy making have argued that the level of state economic resources is among the principal determinants of policy choices.[33] On the surface, the statement above supports the argument of proponents of privatization that states make the decision based on fiscal concerns rather than political patronage. But critics state that the decision is much more complicated and can't be predicted solely by the state's economic resources.

Just like low per capita income, most states with low tax capacity are in the South, and the states with high tax capacity are in the northeast.[34] Proponents of privatization point out that, although limited economic resources may explain the decision to privatize, this fails to explain the fact that the District of Columbia, Hawaii, and New Jersey—all with high tax capacity—have private prisons or export prisoners to private prisons. They also point to states such as Alaska and Wyoming, which are blessed with a wealth of extractable minerals, as to why this explanation is insufficient because these states have private prisons or export prisoners to for-profit prisons despite their wealth. Critics contend that politics and lobbying, not limited economic resources, explain their decision to privatize their prisons. Maine, a wealthy state with a low incarceration rate and private prisons, is often cited as an example of lobbying and a community using prisons for economic development.

When tested, low tax capacity was also found to demonstrate a relationship between the decision to privatize prisons and a state's economic well-being. Because low tax capacity and low per capita income were observed to be related to the decision to privatize, the study does provide some support for advocates of prison privatization. However, when one looks at the fact that privatization is not limited to the South and there are about thirty-one states ranging from low to high tax capacity with private prisons, there has to be some other explanation. Critics ask, if low tax capacity and low per capita income explain a state's choice to privatize and most of the low capacity and low per capita income states are in the South, then why are the West and Midwest so heavily privatized? How do you explain prison privatization in the wealthy states if economic well-being explains policy choices? Why do wealthy states send prisoners to other states even though they have the resources to build their own prisons and house their own prisoners? They send them to other prisons because they do not want private prisons operating in their backyard, and they have been lobbied by for-profit firms to send their prisoners out of state without considering the consequences of sending prisoners away from their families. Finally, the fact that privatization exists outside the South suggests that private prisons exist possibly because of lobbying, which is alleged to influence the privatization decision of many states.

TAX EFFORT

Another variable not mentioned in the standard explanation for why states sought privatization is the tax effort variable. This variable is an indicator of fiscal robustness of the state. According to *Measuring Fiscal Effort and Fiscal Capacity: Sorting Out Some of the Controversies*, "A government's tax effort can be understood as the extent to which it utilizes its tax capacity."[35] Tax effort underscores the extent to which a state is making use of its available tax base.[36] Examining the relationship of tax collections to personal income and tax capacity as calculated by RTS are the two most common ways of measuring tax effort.[37]

Just as with tax capacity, the fifty states diverge sharply in the range of public services their state and local governments must deliver and in the costs of providing them.[38] Here again, the South's tax effort is much higher than states outside the South. This finding supports the proponents of prison privatization who claim that states seek privatization for other legitimate reasons apart from the claims made by opponents of prison privatization.

Tax effort has been described as the burden imposed by levies of state and local governments within each state.[39] When local governments are under fiscal stress, they need to burrow deep into their tax base to produce enough financing.[40] The ability of states to generate revenue through taxes to fund public service is brought into focus when you examine a states' tax effort. This is more pronounced in the South, where privatization is more entrenched. However, the South is not the only region to suffer fiscal problems. For instance, in the 1970s, fiscal crises in several sizeable cities like New York and across the United States caused considerable focus on state budget problems. According to *The Politics of Retrenchment: How Local Governments Manage Fiscal Stress*, "beginning with the fiscal crisis in New York City in 1974 and succeeding crises in Oakland, Cincinnati,

Detroit, Baltimore, and other cities, counties and school districts, the causes, impacts, and management of fiscal stress has become a national concern."[41]

Moreover, most of the attention to adverse fiscal conditions has been focused on large cities.[42] According to some scholars, this is problematic because small localities also experience very similar financial problems and may be even more affected as a result. By examining factors that cause fiscal stress and the myriad measures required to effectively combat those factors, it appears that, in the long run, crises in small cities may be more difficult to combat than those of larger cities.[43] A small city may be disadvantaged in making cuts or raising revenues in comparison with larger cities that have more fiscal elasticity. This point may explain why privatization has made its way to the jail system. At one point, federal and state prisons were the only ones that were amenable to privatization, but now local jails are also private, suggesting that privatization has made its way to the local level. Again, support is found for proponents of privatization who claim that states seek privatization as a viable option to alleviate fiscal stress rather than the reasons provided by critics of privatization efforts. This especially seems true as it concerns the southern region of the country; outside the South, it appears that lobbying and campaign financing have influenced the decision to privatize.

The tax effort variable was tested, and a relationship was found to exist between the privatization decision and the state tax effort. Those states with a high tax effort were more likely to be at risk for privatization than those with normal tax effort. Still again, states in the South were more likely to have a higher tax effort than states outside the South. The cost-savings explanations of proponents of privatization make sense when their logic is applied to the southern region of the country, but it is difficult to explain the level of privatization outside the South. Critics contend that another reason may explain the level of privatization in the South—their lack of unionization. States that are not unionized are more likely to have higher levels of privatization because of the lack of union resistance. When legislators and governors are unimpeded by unions, critics contend, they are more likely to support privatization efforts because of the money contributed to their campaigns by for-profit firms.

Three of the four variables tested in the economic model support the idea that privatization is pursued because of fiscal problems encountered by the states, but this data does not explain why privatization exists outside the South. This, critics contend, is where lobbying and political patronage come into play. Southern states suffer from low tax capacity, high tax effort, low per capita income, and increased correctional expenditures. These states are some of the poorest in the country, and correctional costs compound their fiscal problems. But how do you explain privatization outside the South, where many of the states do not suffer from the same fiscal ailments? For instance, although a state like New Jersey may have a high per capita income and a high tax capacity, it may have tapped out its capacity, requiring it to consider alternatives to alleviate fiscal stress. This appears to support the assertion that fiscal stress drove some states to consider privatizing their prisons, but that does not mean that politics did not play a role in the decision to privatize. It means that there were legitimate concerns for the state, but there were other ways to address prison overcrowding besides privatizing prisons. The bone of contention of critics is the process by which states arrive at the decision to privatize prisons.

Ideological Explanations

The debate to privatize has been ideologically driven. Conservatives argue for privatization on the grounds of promoting limited government involvement and reducing the role of government in citizens' lives. They believe that once the government's role has been reduced in areas like education, transportation, and health care to name a few, the citizens will have more choice, which translates into better service options and increased public sector productivity. Choice introduces competition and, as a result, efficiency and savings materialize because monopoly conditions no longer exist. This argument presupposes that inefficiency and lack of competition exist when the service is publicly run versus privately run. If that supposition is true, privatization can provide better quality and savings because competition promotes efficiency.

The debate to privatize is not confined to savings and quality concerns. Critics contend that conservatives support prison privatization to foster business contacts with their friends who own many of the for-profit firms. There seems to be support for this assertion when examining the state of Tennessee. In 1984, Senator Lamar Alexander, then first-term governor of Tennessee, had agreed to allow the entire Tennessee prison system to be contracted out to CCA. Critics wondered why the governor would approve such a plan, but then found that Thomas Beasley, the former Tennessee Republican Party chairman, had just resigned his post to run CCA. Critics asserted that another interesting reason why the governor agreed to CCA's proposal was that his wife, Honey Alexander, was one of CCA's original investors. Her investment was for $5,000. However, the legislature did not support Governor Alexander's efforts that would have allowed CCA to take over the state's prison system for $178 million a year. In order to legitimatize CCA's proposal to take over the Tennessee state prison system before it was to be submitted to the legislature, Honey Alexander "exchanged her stock for shares in an insurance holding company, which she later sold for $142,000."[44] After Alexander's sale of her CCA stock, enemies of her husband began to focus on the governor's finances.[45]

Another incident suggesting that privatization is more about ideology and not just about costs and quality is the case of Governor Don Sundquist of Tennessee. Governor Don Sundquist was the keynote speaker at ALEC's 26th annual meeting at the Nashville corporate headquarters of CCA.[46] This meeting was comprised of 2,700 attendants and included lawmakers and state and national officials who all gathered to discuss governing and public policy.[47]

Governor Sundquist's attendance would not be a problem in critics' eyes if J. Michael Quinlan, former director of the Federal Bureau of Prisons under Presidents Reagan and Bush and chief operations officer of CCA were not in attendance giving a briefing on the superiority of private prisons versus public prisons. His attendance speaks to the cozy relationship that exists between lawmakers and for-profit prison firms. This is problematic for critics because the same lawmakers are responsible for making laws via ALEC's Criminal Justice Task Force Committee, which sponsors laws that ensure that private prisons' supply levels remain high. Another issue is that Governor Sundquist is a devoted advocate of for-profit prisons and CCA. CCA is headed by Quinlan, whose company is the largest for-profit prison firm in the United States and happens to be in Tennessee, where the prison privatization movement began. Critics believe this makes their relationship unethical; they also find it ironic that Quinlan is addressing "lawmakers and staff about public policy at a conference funded in part by private-prison corporations and held in Nashville, home to CCA."[48]

In the face of these findings, ideological variables were tested to see if there was support for critics' assertion that the decision to privatize is affected by ideologically driven politicians looking to reward politically connected friends who own for-profit prisons.

To see if they support critics' arguments that privatization is more about political patronage than costs and quality, I tested political ideology, which includes state ideology and citizen ideology, as well as control of state legislatures and the governor's political party. Citizen and state ideology are tested because citizens play a role in whether the states seek certain privatization initiatives. For instance, the legislator in Tennessee defeated Governor's Alexander efforts to privatize the entire Tennessee prison system in part because of the opposition of citizens. It is possible that if the citizenry identified with a conservative philosophy that they would support such an initiative. It is also possible that they may not support such an initiative regardless of their ideological identification. The same reasoning can be ascribed to state ideology, which examines the attitudes of state officials on a liberal-conservative continuum.

Although state ideology may appear to be the same as control of the legislature, control of legislature does not capture the ideology of local officials; thus, state ideology serves as a good variable to assess the ideological attitude of public officials. It should be noted that privatization is not a solely conservative argument; there are cases in which liberal citizens and legislators support privatization. However, most proposals to support privatization are orchestrated by conservatives. For example, the Grace Commission, the brainchild of Presidents Reagan and Bush that supported privatization and championed school vouchers and choice is an example of the type of initiatives conservatives support.

CONTROL OF LEGISLATURE

Critics contend that for-profit firms make campaign contributions to conservative legislators to influence sentencing policy. For-profit firms vehemently deny these accusations, "Yet, both CCA and Wackenhut are major contributors to the American Legislative Exchange Council (ALEC), a Washington DC based public policy organization that supports conservative legislators."[49] This is problematic because over 40 percent of all state legislators hold membership in ALEC, "representing a serious force in state politics."[50] According to *Prison Privatization and the Use of Incarceration,* "one of ALEC's primary functions is the development of model legislation that advances conservative principles, such as privatization."[51] A point that captures critics' concerns is that ALEC's Criminal Justice Task Force "has developed and helped to successfully implement in many states 'tough on crime' initiatives including 'Truth in Sentencing' and 'Three Strikes' laws."[52]

Another conflicting aspect for legislators who are members of ALEC is that corporations provide most of the funding for ALEC's operating budget. In addition, they attempt to influence ALEC's agenda by serving on policy task forces that focus on criminal justice policy. Unsurprisingly, two of ALEC's biggest contributors are CCA and Wackenhut (now known as the GEO Group). These "big two" have members on the Criminal Justice Task Force. Additionally, ALEC recognizes its contributors via the President's List for contributions during its States and National Policy Summit. This is not an unusual practice, but it is problematic because Wackenhut sponsored the 1999 summit. This is only the tip of the iceberg regarding how interconnected the prison for-profit industry is with ALEC. For instance, many past "co-chairs of the Criminal Justice Task Force have included Brad Wiggins, then Director of Business Development at CCA and now a Director of Customer Relations, and John Rees, a CCA vice president."[53] "By funding and participating in ALEC's Criminal Justice Task Force, private prison companies can directly influence legislation related to sentencing—in this case, harsh sentencing laws sending more people to prison longer."[54]

There are six factors that are more likely to influence the legislators when they make decisions on policy: (1) their party and party leaders, (2) committees, (3) staff, (4) lobbyists representing private interest groups and executive agencies, (5) the governor, and (6) constituents in their legislative districts.[55] From the discussion above, critics contend that if the legislature is controlled by Republicans, the state is more likely to support prison privatization. They point to the relationship between ALEC members, who are mostly conservative, and the amount of interaction between them and for-profit providers that serve on the Criminal Justice Task Force with them and make policy recommendations. Contributions from for-profit firms made to these conservative legislators are also scrutinized and are offered up as the rationale as to why states controlled by Republicans will be amenable to prison privatization.

These variables were tested and the findings demonstrated that the ideology of the legislature was not a factor concerning the decision to privatize. A Democrat-controlled legislature was just as likely to support privatization as a Republican-controlled legislature. This finding contradicts the idea that conservatively controlled legislatures are more likely to consider prison privatization than liberally controlled legislature. The finding is not consistent with the literature and supports the claim that privatization is sought as a viable alternative to alleviate fiscal stress.

GOVERNOR'S PARTY

Partisanship is a key variable in the governors' relationship with the legislatures.[56] Additionally, if the governor's party controls the legislature, then partisan conflicts can be curtailed, and the governor likely will have more success in implementing his or her agenda.[57] When there is divided government, the governor is more likely to face partisan battles when making policy. Furthermore, "when the party majorities in the legislative houses are from the same political party as the governor, legislators' support for the governor's legislative program may be impossible to disentangle from partisan voting behavior."[58] If the governor has an oppositional party in one or both houses of the legislature, he or she is likely to have less influence over the agenda of the state.[59]

75

Opponents of privatization contend that conservative governors are much more likely to push through privatization initiatives than liberal governors. They point to the ALEC meetings and the relationship many of the governors have with the for-profit firm's representatives, who share membership on policy-making task forces with governors. However, the legislature's composition determines the policy options the governor will pursue. Although governors are not able to get privatization initiatives through the houses without assistance, they can be a powerful advocate for privatization because they can take their message directly to the people and the media to pressure the legislature for their policy preference.

Conservative governors such as Bush (TX), Engler (MI), Rendell (PA), Ryan (IL), Thompson (WI), Schwarzenegger (CA), and Whitman (NJ) have all championed privatization as a cure for fiscal woes during their tenures in office. Each felt that privatization would help close budget gaps by saving money and improving services. But critics contend that conservative governors pursue privatization to reward politically connected politicians, contributors to their campaigns, and sometimes their spouses. For instance, former governor of New Jersey and Former Administrator of the U.S. Environmental Protection Agency (EPA) Christine Todd Whitman oversaw a proposed cleanup project worth $7.2 million in Denver for a property owned by Citigroup, an investment firm in which Whitman's husband owns $100,000 to $250,000 in company shares. Her husband's company received the contract for this cleanup, and many point to Whitman's influence as the EPA Director as the reason why her husband's company received this contract. Critics point to this kind of patronage by conservatives to explain why governors and politicians seek privatization.

A test was performed to see whether Republican governors were more likely to support privatization than liberal or independent governors. There was no relationship between the decision to privatize and a Republican governor. Again, the findings contradict critics' claims that a Republican governor would more likely support the decision to privatize. Based on this finding, it appears that partisanship is not a predictor regarding the privatization decision. Is it correct to assume that privatization transcends boundaries?[60] It appears

76

that there may be support for this belief because privatization of prisons has not been confined to states with Republican governors only; there have been privatization efforts led by Democratic governors for the purpose of using privatization to alleviate fiscal stress. The only unsubstantiated difference between Republicans and Democrats when considering privatization is that Democrats appear to pursue it to alleviate fiscal stress and Republicans pursue it (the evidence is circumstantial) as a means to reward or return a political favor. Again, evidence is found to support proponents of privatization who aver that privatization is not a partisan argument but a pragmatic solution to address fiscal concerns, increased correctional costs, and costs savings—all of which would greatly improve the fiscal robustness of states that have been handicapped by inefficiency. As a result of their inefficiency, the citizens are being underserved because the government is wasting money; thus privatization is a viable solution. Proponents of privatization argue that when the governor argues for privatization, he or she argues for pragmatic versus political reasons.

POLITICAL IDEOLOGY

Political ideology has been defined as the aggregation of the issue preferences of a state's population, that is, an instrument developed to measure each citizen in that states political ideology, which can be placed on a liberal-conservative continuum—a scale from 0–100. The closer to 100, the more liberal the state.[61] In addition, this concept is meant to characterize the degree to which the citizens of a state will support liberal versus conservative positions and candidates for political office.[62] This point is very important because it speaks to how receptive the citizens of the state are to privatization. Research shows that citizens who are identified as or identify with being conservative are more likely to support privatization efforts.

Not a lot is known about prison privatization efforts between 1979 and 1984, but during the initial efforts to privatize prisons in 1979 and 1984, Florida, Tennessee, and Texas were the first states to embrace privatization. According to the political culture typology, Tennessee and Texas are states with a traditionalist political culture. Citizens from traditionalist states support the idea that government should have a limited role in society.[63] They see this as the most appropriate role for government because the government is only necessary to meet the needs of those in power.[64] The South has been identified with this type of culture, and it is in the South that prison privatization efforts were initiated. Although political culture is mentioned here, it has a much wider political significance and will be discussed in more detail in the section on political explanations.

The Republican Party initiated the belief that a criminal act is an individual responsibility, and they pressed the view for decades.[65] Their point is that the government has been unable to rehabilitate criminals through social action, and the money spent on rehabilitation has been astronomical and wasteful; thus, the private sector should take this responsibility because the government has not been successful. By pressing this perspective, conservatives attempt to sway citizens who are amenable to limited government involvement to support prison privatization. Additionally, this perspective corresponds to the presumably greater Republican support for a range of social-control programs—longer periods of incarceration, expanded police services in local communities, fewer restraints on law-enforcement officers, and so on.[66] Moreover, conservatives are able to successfully argue for prison privatization in the states characterized as individualistic and traditionalist because the citizens in these states believe that politicical power is inherited and politicians have a family obligation to govern.[67] The argument by conservatives in support of prison privatization also gained traction as a result of three factors: (a) the feelings of hostility and desires for revenge that criminals arouse in their victims and those who sympathize with the victims, (b) abstract normative philosophies, ideologies, and religious beliefs regarding punishment, and (c) prevailing theories of crime causation.[68]

According to an article in the *American Journal of Political Science,* "Democracy requires a strong correspondence between popular preferences, the ideological orientations of elected representatives, and government policies."[69] Two concepts are essential to their analyses; one is state citizen ideology, "generally conceived as the mean position on a liberal-conservative continuum of the 'active electorate' in a state,"[70] and the second is state government ideology, "the mean position on the same continuum of the elected public officials in a state, weighted according to the power they have over public policy decisions."[71]

In ideological explanations, legislature control, governor's party, and political ideology—which is bifurcated into citizen ideology and state ideology—are included in this discussion because they speak to the partisan nature of states and how policy making is impacted by the party in power and the citizenry. Throughout the privatization literature, critics contend that conservatives advocate for private involvement in government because it promotes efficiency and competition. With spiraling correctional expenditures, overcrowded prison populations, and increasing crime, the call for private involvement in the correctional crisis became louder. With the calls to privatize, conservatives were also able to shift the penal philosophy in the United States from a rehabilitative model to a punitive model, especially with the media overexposing the crack cocaine epidemic and attendant violence. Most politicians were boxed in by the "tough on crime" climate created by conservatives; thus, they have been unable to stem the correctional cost associated with this new punitive penal philosophy because no politician wanted to be viewed as soft on crime. As a result, citizens became more amenable to prison privatization.

Because it has been argued that political ideology impacts a states' decision to privatize its prisons, citizen ideology and state ideology were tested to see if a relationship existed between the privatization decision and citizen ideology and state ideology. Evidence was found to support the idea that the more conservative the citizens are in the state, the more agreeable they are to privatization as an alternative to solve government problems. However, state ideology was not a predictor in the decision to privatize prisons. These findings suggest that the citizenry was more important than their representatives in determining the policy choice concerning prison privatization. This explanation is in line with the efforts of citizens in rural communities to secure prisons for economic development. On the other hand, maybe the representatives and the media were more important in deciding the privatization decision because they were the ones framing the argument, bashing the government, and creating the fear around crime that lead to many of the "get tough on crime" initiatives that placed a tremendous amount of pressure on state budgets because of the amount of people arrested.

The idea that if the citizens were conservative, privatization efforts would be more welcome in that state is supported by my findings, and this suggests that citizens supporting limited government involvement and pursuing prisons as economic development drove the decision to privatize, not political patronage as critics of prison privatization assert. It also suggests that conservatives were effective in disparaging the government's ability to manage prisons effectively and efficiently.

Political Explanations

The final variables that affected many states were the crime rate, neighboring states' privatization behavior, political culture, and prison capacity. Here, too, these variables possibly played a significant role in the states' privatization decision, but they have been omitted from the standard discussion as to why states privatized their prisons, just as the economic and ideological explanations were. These variables were tested to see if they revealed any deviation from the standard (piecemeal) explanations of prison privatization decisions. Critics introduce the political model issues in the standard literature, and this study builds on their assertions.[72]

CRIME RATES

The imprisonment surge can be traced to several prominent factors.[73] For one, "fear was initially aroused by a substantial increase in the major 'index' crimes (homicides, assaults, robberies, rape, burglary, theft, and arson) reported to police in the late 1960s and early 1970s."[74] The public has continued to believe that crime has been increasing; their fear of crime has remained high, and the media has exacerbated public fears with overreporting of violence in the inner cities. Moreover, during this time period, the public remained pessimistic that crime, unlike other social issues, could be reduced."[75]

As a result, in the 1980s the fear of crime and rampant drug abuse in upscale communities was elevated each election year because of the attention politicians and the media gave to crime and drug problems.[76] Critics imply that during the 1980s the public altered its focus (or, more correctly, had its focus shifted by the media) to violent crime, even as the violent crime rate declined:

Politicians harangue on the street crime problem because it is a safe issue. It is easy to cast in simple terms of good versus evil and no powerful constituency is directly offended by a campaign against street crime. Some politicians also use street crime to divert attention away from other pressing social problems— such as the threat of nuclear war, unemployment, high living costs, and the economy—all of which persistently top the list of public concerns. Measures to solve these problems would require changes that would offend powerful interest groups.[77]

The politicalization of crime continued with the war on drugs. In an analysis of the nation's war on drugs published by the National Council on Crime and Delinquency, the author points out that the drug problem received similar treatment from the media:

The Reagan administration initiated a "War on Drugs" in the early 1980s. The Bush administration appointed a "Drug Czar," and recently offered a major plan to remove the "scourge" of drugs from the American landscape. The media have reported on the violence occurring in our inner cities and on cocaine-source nations like Colombia. The public is bombarded with news about drugs, like the drug death of sports figure Len Bias and the confessions of celebrities about personal struggles with substance abuse.[78]

The drug war initiated by politicians also stimulated a movement toward more punitive sentencing policies for drug dealers, such as mandatory sentencing, which has led to prison overcrowding and increased correctional expenditures. Politicians—especially conservative politicians affiliated with ALEC—utilized crime rates to justify stiffer sentences and to argue for the steady and increased use of privatization in corrections.

In their steady and unrelenting tirades on the crime and drug problems, politicians have squabbled that steady and dramatic expansion of prison populations is absolutely necessary to maintain a safe society. Politicians assert that increases in imprisonment are positive signs, and it symbolizes that the nation is more and more intolerant of criminals and their antisocial and too-often violent behavior. Moreover, they purport that increased use of imprisonment in particular and punishment in general has reduced crime.

With the politicalization of the crime rate, the frenzy created by the politicians in conjunction with the media, the "war on drugs" and "get tough on crime" campaigns, it is not surprising that prison populations skyrocketed along with costs to manage prisons. As a result, the crime rate should be a predictor as to why states sought prison privatization. When the crime rate variable was tested to see if a relationship existed between privatization and an increasing crime rate, a relationship was found between the two—that is, states with a high crime rate were more likely to support prison privatization. Again, this evidence supports proponents of privatization who claim that states seek privatization when they can no longer afford to pay for services or when they are no longer able to manage the service and something has to be done outside of the normal way of conducting business. In many cases, privatization is the answer to a state's problems. On the other hand, critics point to the fact that, in many cases, the crime rate went down and stayed down for a number of years, but the imprisonment rate continued to increase along with privatization of prisons. How do you explain this phenomenon critics of prison privatization contend? They point their fingers at ALEC's lobbying for probation and parole reduction, which means more prisoners go back to jail for technical violations of their parole and probation. My findings regarding the crime rate's linked to the privatization decision do not explain the increased use of privatization as the crime rate went down and stayed down. As a result, I looked for answers outside of the broader explanations I used to explain the states privatization decisions.

NEIGHBORING STATES' PRIVATIZATION BEHAVIOR

The neighboring states privatization behavior variable speaks to the idea of regional diffusion or policy innovation. *Regional diffusion* models emphasize the influence of nearby states, assuming that states emulate their neighbors when confronted with policy problems or innovations.[79] In addition, a state government innovation has been defined as a "program or policy, which is new to [the state] adopting it."[80] The central research question about state innovation is: "What causes a government to adopt a new program or policy?"[81]

There are two fundamental answers as to why states adopt certain policies.[82] The first is the *internal determinants model,* which looks at the internal political, economic, and social factors that lead a state to innovate.[83] The second is *regional diffusion*, which emphasizes the influence of nearby states and assumes that states emulate their neighbors when confronted with policy problems.[84]

Studies by various scholars have found that policy innovations tend to disseminate based on a pattern in which regional leader states initiate the cues for later adopters.[85] In other words, fellow leaders adopt policies that seem to work in other states. Additionally, this idea underscores Frances Stokes Berry's and William D. Berry's conception of regional diffusion, which asserts that "a state is more likely to adopt an innovation as the number of neighboring states adopts the policy."[86] Research shows that bordering states are most likely to share common political cultures and socioeconomic characteristics and are viewed by state leaders as the best laboratories for innovations.[87]

With the preceding research in place, the neighboring states' privatization variable was tested to see if prison privatization occurred because of policy diffusion. The neighboring state privatization variable was found to be a predictor in the states decision to privatize. As stated before, the test predicted a state's likelihood of seeking privatization; it does not determine if the state will privatize. Again, evidence was found to support the idea that privatization was sought by states because they saw other states successfully employ this strategy to address prison overcrowding, increased correctional costs, and fiscal woes associated with the increasing inmate population. The evidence from the states' view suggests that other decisions drove the decision to privatize besides costs and quality concerns that are considered in the standard explanations as the reasons why states privatized their prisons.

POLITICAL CULTURE

Political culture has been described as "the particular pattern of orientation to political action in which each political system is imbedded."[88] Political cultures differ in beliefs and values concerning the opposite goals of a political system, the function of political parties in achieving those goals, and the activities of citizens, elites, and professional politicians in politics.[89]

Political culture has been divided into three subcultures that surfaced from different past migration patterns of U.S. citizens. In the traditionalist political culture, the objective of the political system is one of maintaining the existing order. There is low interparty competition and public policies and actions are determined primarily by the elite.[90] In the *individualistic* political culture, the political arena is viewed as a marketplace for ideas and actions; political actions are determined by public demands. Lastly, in the *moralistic* culture, the objective of the political system is to achieve the broadest good for the community with or without public pressure.

For individuals, the state of residence is an important predictor of partisanship and ideological identification, independent of their demographic characteristics.[91] Scholars find that geographic location may have more relevance as a source of opinion than previously believed.[92] They declare that one indication of the importance of state culture is that state effects on partisanship and ideology account for about half of the variance in state voting in recent presidential elections.[93]

In the ideological discussion, political culture served as a backdrop for ideological underpinnings that drove the decision to privatize. Here it is examined to see if individualistic political culture is related to the states decision to privatize. States with an individualistic political culture were found to have a relationship with the privatization decision of the state; thus, those states that are identified as having individualistic political cultures were more likely to pursue prison privatization. This is yet another argument in favor of those who contend that privatization is sought to alleviate fiscal pressures and not because of political patronage; in this case, the political culture of the citizens speaks to their amenability to reducing the role of government and allowing market conditions to prevail. Those states in which the citizens are identified as individualistic appreciate privatization initiatives as an option to solve government problems.

PRISON CAPACITY

An outraged and crime-weary citizenry demanded that dangerous criminals be locked away for life. As a result, politicians across the United States called for tougher laws, such as mandatory sentencing. This call for tougher sentences wreaked havoc on the criminal justice system, driving prison capacity well above normal levels and increasing correctional costs by 500 percent in some states. Chief Justice Rehnquist contends that "mandatory minimum sentences are a good example of the law of unintended consequences."[94] Additionally, mandatory sentences have led to an inordinate increase in the federal prison population and huge expenditures will be required to build new prison space.[95]

Prison overcrowding has become such a problem that in 1990, about one-fifth of the nation's state prisons were ordered by the courts to reduce their populations.[96] Likewise, the nation's local jails were not immune to the overcrowding problem—approximately 9 percent were under similar sanctions.[97] Many state corrections officials say that prison overcrowding results when mandatory sentencing detracts from their ability to identify and put away the violent criminals, "yet expanding the federal mandatory sentencing approach to the state-level with its accompanying demands for more prisons—is precisely the approach taken in the Senate crime bill [the Violent Crime Control and Law Enforcement Act of 1994] and by proponents of a general crime crackdown."[98] At the end of 1997, "state prisons were 15% above their highest capacity, Federal Prisons 19% above their rated capacity." Additionally, the report shows that "California is operating at over twice its highest reported capacity (206%)."[99]

In 1992, the Justice Department, under the watch of the Bush administration, released a position paper entitled "The Case for More Incarceration," which argued that prison was cheaper than the alternatives, and violent crime had been declining since the government began locking people up in prison. Most importantly, the position paper attempted to justify the Bush administration's policy of getting tough on crime by arguing that most violent crime is committed by parolees and other individuals previously ensnared in the criminal justice system.[100] In other words, advocates of incarceration argue that because most violent crimes are committed by parolees, longer sentences or mandatory minimum sentences are needed to incapacitate those individuals for longer time periods, which will also reduce the crime rate. However, as Justice Rehnquist cogently posited, mandatory sentencing has unintended consequences. Prisons began to bulge and fill beyond capacity with nonviolent "drug criminals" caught in the war on drugs' "weed and seed" strategy, many of them first time offenders. According to the Department of Justice, "weed and seed" is a focused multiagency strategy conducted in a targeted area with an emphasis on controlling violent crime, drug trafficking, and drug-related crime. An unintended consequence of this policy was that violent repeat offenders were pushed out of the prison doors early or never imprisoned in the first place.[101]

With state correctional budgets exploding, the efficacy of mandatory prison terms for drug offenders is being questioned.[102] Many lawmakers are calling for repeal or revision of the laws to reduce the stress being placed on budgets. However, Florida State Representative Tracy Stafford said in the *Florida News-Sentinel*, "reducing mandatory minimum sentences will take some nerve in the Legislature because you're going to subject yourself to an attack that you are soft on crime."[103] The idea of being "soft on crime" serves as the crux of the problem of prison overcrowding and the issue of capacity. Politicians have created a climate of fear and punitiveness that they cannot undo. As a result, crowding has not abated, and the problems associated with prison overcrowding, such as prisoner violence, health issues, and riots, continue as states grapple with pressing issues of decreasing budgets and rising correctional costs.

The issue of prison overcrowding has had severe budget and policy implications for decision makers. Budgeting decisions center on how to manage increasing correctional expenditures resulting from increasing prison populations in a time of reduced resources brought on by prison overcrowding. Courts have mandated that states do something about their crowding problems and have passed legislation enabling states to choose a private alternative to handle prison capacity problems. As a consequence, some policy makers faced with prison overcrowding have chosen privatization to reduce the stress being placed on their budgets.

The prison capacity variable was tested to see if a relationship existed between those states with prison capacity problems and their decision to privatize. The prison capacity variable was found to not have a relationship with the states' privatization decision. This outcome was unexpected because the capacity problems that states were experiencing drove many courts to pass legislation to allow those states to pursue private options to address the capacity problems, which bred crime, violence, and unhealthy conditions in prisons. The findings here require that further research be conducted to explore why states privatized their prisons.

In each case, several variables were found to have a positive relationship with the privatization decision, and several were found to be unrelated to the privatization decision. The variables that had a positive relationship with the privatization decision support the claims made by proponents of privatization that states sought privatization as an option to address the government's failure to resolve the correctional crisis. The findings in this study would seem to support their claims in some instances, but in other cases, it does not. Because of the mixed results, additional research was conducted to corroborate my findings.

What's the Real Reason Behind State Prison Privatization?

A forthcoming dissertation from Yijia Jing supports my argument that the debate must be expanded from a cost and quality one to a much broader debate before definitive claims are made regarding why states privatize their prisons. He asserts that expanding the debate identifies key variables in the empirical analysis used to explain the states privatization decision.[104] Jing points out that there may be other explanations beyond those I identified that explain why states privatized.[105]

After delving further into the literature, I found several reasons why states sought to privatize their prisons. In each set of arguments, there are legitimate explanations as to why states sought prison privatization, and there are legitimate challenges to the findings in both set of arguments. However, once one moves beyond the standard explanations and broader state-level explanations, more sinister factors come into play. Critics contend that the public's attention is being diverted from the real reasons why states seek privatization and, because of this, the darker agenda of prison privatization is kept under the radar while researchers attempt to prove an observed relationship between the standard and the broader explanations. Opponents of prison privatization contend that the public should be looking at the vested interest that accompanies the privatization of prisons. For instance, critics point out that once prisons are privatized, the private firms build "spec" (speculative) prisons—prisons built without the state's involvement in hopes of landing a contract with the state where the prison is built or with other states. Private prisons, especially spec prisons, import and export prisoners. Spec prisons are not under contract with the state in which they are physically located nor did they have to be until states began to pass laws regulating these prisons. They were like any other business setting up shop. Since they were built without the involvement of the states in which they resided, they were not precluded from exporting or importing inmates. They could export prisoners with the contracting state's permission to another one of their facilities. Also, because private prison stock is publicly traded, they pursue practices that maximize shareholder wealth. Private prisons exploit prison labor. The legislators in rural communities become dependent on prisoners because they help the state meet population requirements, which impact their economic and political power. Private prisons are also used as an economic development tool in rural communities.

The standard explanation and broader state explanations pale in comparison to the more disturbing explanations critics point out as to why states seek prison privatization—explanations that seem to be a better barometer of state privatization decisions. Prison privatization has become a billion-dollar industry, and opponents of prison privatization contend that the standard and broader explanations are a diversion for what's really driving the decision to privatize prisons. They assert that the American public is being sold a "bill of goods" concerning why states seek prison privatization.

Chapter Four

Speculative Prisons

Introduction

It is clear that private prisons have a vested interest to incarcerate. How else would they make money if they had no prisoners to house? But the idea that prison privatization is an effort to reinvent government is specious; private prisons are there to make money and to increase their market share, like any other business. Building a speculative prison—one built on the promise of needing more space for more prisoners—contradicts our efforts to cut down on crime and help members of society become productive and law-abiding.

Speculative prisons reinforce the idea that for-profit prisons are an economic opportunity for rural communities because they serve as an emerging market for potential investors looking for new markets to exploit. Using prisons as an economic development strategy is ironic when one considers that for years prisons have been shunned in communities concerned with the perception of having a prison in their backyard. In the past, the "not in my back yard" (NIMBY) attitude always met any proposal to build a prison in just about any community in the United States. The rise of prison privatization in the 1980s brought a more favorable view of prisons to communities looking for economic development opportunities. A new attitude toward prisons, coupled with unprecedented job loss in rural communities, paved the way for more prison building. Prison expansion was facilitated by tax subsidies in many rural communities, a strategy employed to ensure that these prisons would locate there. Seventy-three percent of the private prisons that located in these communities received a subsidy "from a local, state and/or federal government source."[1]

As prison populations continued to swell in the 1980s due to the punitive climate and the need to create jobs, the for-profit providers began to explore ways to exploit the new amenability to prisons. The economic development opportunity prisons provided in rural communities was the impetus for-profit prisons needed to enter this market and expand their operations. Spec prisons were built mostly in rural, white communities with high unemployment. These prisons were strategically situated in communities in which citizens were unwilling to pay additional taxes to build prisons, places where they could not afford to build additional prisons, and places were jobs were needed. Ironically, for rural communities hemorrhaging from job loss, NIMBY no longer had significance; prisons became welcome additions to replace jobs that have been exported abroad. At one time, spec prisons were very prominent in driving economic development decisions in rural communities; however, many states began to pass laws banning speculative prisons, and these prisons are no longer being built because of a few high-profile problems they have encountered. For instance, Youngstown, Ohio, is the exemplar of what can and did go wrong in many of the speculative prisons. The Youngstown case, which was briefly discussed in chapter one and will be discussed later in this chapter, introduces the reasons why spec prisons need to be regulated.

Speculative building also illustrates the process that went into building these prisons and the economics that drove the decision to build. For instance, builders of speculative prisons would look at the state's fiscal problems, crime rate, the citizens' attitude toward raising taxes to build prisons, and the state's overcrowding problems. Once they compiled this information, they would determine if the state could use another prison. If the answer was yes, they built the prisons without the state's involvement. Typically, speculative prison building was aimed at rural communities ravaged by massive job loss and looking for ways to revitalize the community. Prisons became more appealing to these residents considering the depressed state of their communities and the state's willingness to subsidize the prisons. In some instances, when the states were unwilling to subsidize the private prisons and taxpayers were unwilling to allow bonds to finance prisons, the for-profit providers solicited financing from private entities—a practice which radically altered the ways correctional facilities were financed and built. For example, government-issued bonds were replaced by private-lease purchase arrangements, and these arrangements were designed by investment firms such as E. F. Hutton, Merrill Lynch, Morgan Stanley and Company, and Shearson Lehman Brothers.[2] For-profit prisons providers covered just about every base they needed to make sure these speculative prisons would get built. The involvement of Wall Street investment bankers in the financing of prisons clearly supports my assertion that the debate surrounding whether or not prisons should be privatized is more complicated than the public has been led to believe. The debate is not the same once it is examined from the profit motive lens. Wall Street investment bankers are not involved in financing prison construction to make our society safer; they are in the business exclusively to make a profit. They obviously understood the cliché "if we build them, they will come," which has its roots in space-utilization theory. Space-utilization theory suggests that once the prison is built to relieve overcrowding, it has the opposite effect because prison population increases to fill this void. There will be no need to change sentencing policy because these prisons have all the space they need to house those sentenced under laws such as mandatory sentencing and truth-in-sentencing. It is only when there are space problems that policy makers revisit sentencing policy.

To ensure that they would always have a steady flow of prisoners when factors advantageous to incarceration were not available in the state the spec prison operated in, these corporations went as far as soliciting other states for prisoners when there was a downward turn in crime rate in their host state. For instance, Hawaii has exported prisoners to Texas because the state refused to build additional prisons; Texas solicited Hawaii for prisoners because it has the largest number of private prisons. What are the implications of importing and exporting prisoners? What happens when these prisons are built and the crime rate goes down? Well, this question has been answered: spec prisons solicit out-of-state prisoners to fill their empty beds. Are private agencies likely to lobby states to allow them to import prisoners? Critics say yes, and this book addresses those claims.

States that allow private agencies to build these types of prisons assume a great deal of risk. This is reinforced by the example of Youngstown, Ohio. Youngstown received prisoners from Washington, DC, that were thought to be minimum security prisoners, but they were actually maximum security prisoners. These prisoners were placed in the general population in the Youngstown facility and, predictably, they killed a few prisoners and then escaped from the privately managed facility. This created a public relations nightmare for CCA, which ran the prison. Once the prisoners escaped, the debate centered on who should pay for their capture. Should it be the private prison, the state of Ohio, or Washington, DC? Of course, the private provider felt that the state of Ohio should recover the prisoners and absorb the expenses to capture them. The problem with this scenario is that the speculative prison was built without the state's involvement, but the state ended up being responsible for what happened in this private facility. How should the state handle this scenario? Another concern voiced by critics of privatization is when the prison does not bring the necessary jobs promised or there are not enough prisoners to fill the bed spaces, does the state begin to look for ways to secure prisoners to meet its contractual obligations? In others words, does the state become more punitive in its sentencing policies to meet its per diem obligation to the private agency? When a prison is built speculatively, states are somewhat forced to use the existing facility because state officials cannot justify to taxpayers building a new prison using public funds when one is available that was built by private funds.

History of Speculative Prisons

Before the history of speculative prisons is discussed, it is helpful to reiterate the attributes of speculative prisons. A "spec" prison is privately built, without a contract or the assistance of an agency. The prison can take in prisoners from other states as it expands or if it loses its original contract with the state in which it resides. In fact, the prison may only contain out-of-state prisoners. Usually, these prisons are built to help the surrounding community financially.[3]

The main players at the forefront of speculative prison building (or prisons without borders, as they have been described) was CCA and the Geo Group Inc.(formerly Wackenhut). CCA has been described as the industry leader in the area of building speculative prisons. According to Governing Magazine, "in one of the earliest and most infamous experiences with speculative building, a handful of Texas Counties built new prisons in 1991, only to see them sit vacant."[4] Most observers feel that the vacant prisons in Texas would have discouraged private operators from building; however, speculative prisons afforded private vendors the option of importing prisoners from states such as Wisconsin and North Carolina without the interference of hosting states. This was possible because initially speculative prisons were not regulated.

The process states used to award contracts prior to speculative prison building consisted of soliciting proposals from contractors willing to meet the requirements of the state's contract. As the demand for additional space continued to grow, some for-profit providers began to recognize the potential profitability this industry could offer their businesses; they stopped waiting for states to issue requests for proposals, and they began to assume the risk of building private prisons without a contract from the state. These companies were so certain that they would be able to fill these prisons that they built these prisons without a corrections department guarantee of prisoners; thus, the moniker "spec" prison was derived because these types of prisons were built as speculative endeavors by private corporations. Once built, they operated as any other business would. For example, they advertised their prisons to corrections agencies suffering from overcrowding problems and those unwilling or unable to build additional prisons. The for-profit firms that were successful in recruiting prisoners from other states to house in their spec facilities held prisoners from an array of different state agencies out of state and within the state. Their ability to market nationwide may explain the ease at which they were able to secure investment capital from such investors as E. F. Hutton and Merrill Lynch.

The idea of building speculative prisons is not a new one: "during the mid-1980s, a number of small correctional firms were buying or building detention facilities with an eye to offering the beds to a regional market."[5] Not surprisingly, the state of Texas has led the way in speculative building with twenty-three of these types of prisons in the state.[6] At least nine of these facilities house prisoners from outside the state.[7] An interesting point about speculative prisons is that they may not house *any* prisoners from the states in which they are situated. In many cases, the only dealings they have with the state are their obligation to pay corporate taxes, and many sidestep these taxes by creating REITs. During the early stages of speculative building, for-profit proprietors did not even need a license to construct or operate a prison in the state. It was not until several high-profile incidents, such as the prisoner beatings captured on tape in Brazoria County outside of Houston and the murders in the Youngstown facility, that state legislatures realized that they needed to establish regulatory systems to govern private prisons, especially speculative prisons.

The number of states that exported and imported prisoners, as well as those that banned this practice, was quite numerous. During the height of prison privatization, twenty states and the District of Columbia exported prisoners to speculative prisons, and fourteen states with speculative prisons imported prisoners. North Carolina placed a moratorium on importing prisoners, and North Dakota banned the exportation of prisoners to out of state prisons. Given the fact that family contact is a key factor in helping inmates reintegrate into their communities, I find it surprising that states exported prisoners as much as they did. I would think that recidivism would be at the front of their minds when they considered exporting prisoners, but it obviously was not when one looks at the level of exportation that took place doing the height of speculative prison building. Speculative prisons are clearly interested in profit; why else would a prison take on prisoners from other states with the potential inter-jurisdictional problems that accompany such a practice?

Exporting and importing prisoners is a very lucrative business for for-profit prison providers. The business is so lucrative, in fact, that for-profit firms that build speculative prisons gave $72,150 to Georgia lawmakers and political parties in the 2000 election cycle. Georgia politicians were not the only beneficiary of this largesse; according to a report by the Institute on Money in State Politics, during that same election cycle, for-profit providers of prisons contributed $1.2 million to lawmakers in fourteen southeastern states.[8]

Speculative building is also facilitated by the fact that there is no contractual relationship between prison operators and governments of the states in which they operate. The significance of this point is that the for-profit providers of prisons can withhold information relevant to public safety. They also can sidestep requests to disclose relevant safety data. As a result, many states have exported prisoners to these prisons under the belief that these prisons are safe because there is no record indicating otherwise. Spec prisons drove the exportation and importation of prisoners and incorporated these practices into their marketing strategy, never considering the impact exporting and importing prisoners has on recidivism, the host community, and the sending community. Their only concern was maximizing profits and shareholder wealth.

The unwillingness to disclose information by private prisons was one of the main strategies used to keep their prisons appealing and to make bold claims about superior safety and efficiency as compared to public prisons. Private prisons are protected from criticism because these claims can only be substantiated by their records, which they keep hidden from public scrutiny. While the phenomenon of building speculative prisons seems to have subsided, private prisons continue to thrive, although their stock prices have been taking a beating. On the other hand, it makes sense that private prisons continue to thrive when one considers the fact that many of the speculative prisons were built for economic development purposes.

When one considers the fact that, in the United States, the impetus for privatization has been the partnership between political officials and private management groups, it is not surprising that for-profit prisons are surviving in an era of low stock prices and massive job loss in rural communities. Why have they survived? Well, elected officials perceive privatization as reducing the costs of government. This perception has teeth and has served as an impetus for speculative prison building in the 1990s. The building of speculative facilities also shifted the for-profit prison arena from a demand- to a supply-generated approach, which creates a vested interest for the speculative facilities. When there was no demand for their services in their respective states, they were driven to solicit prisoners from other states because they are paid on a per diem basis. The shift to a supply-driven approach meant private firms had to be proactive in securing prisoners. Not only have they been proactive in importing prisoners, but they have also lobbied for stiffer sentencing policies and contributed to conservative and liberal politicians to pass legislation favorable to their industry. In addition, speculative ventures in the for-profit prison industry and the health care industry are both market-driven and they rely on marketing rather than relying on their record of providing quality. For the most part, speculative prisons can be described as a fad that was endemic to the United States, and they have not had a lot of success. On the other hand, speculative prisons did solve many states' overcrowding problems. For states under court order to resolve overcrowding problems, speculative prisons were a godsend.

Although speculative prisons have been described as unsuccessful, they have managed to secure their permanency in many cases by locating in rural communities in need of jobs and by lobbying legislators in those rural communities to pass laws favorable to their industry. By aligning their interest with the interest of the communities that they situate in, they have created dependence that no legislator in his or her right mind would dare challenge. It is not feasible for a legislator to shut down a prison in a rural community. Speculative prisons have proven successful for their stockholders, but they have not necessarily proven that they are better than publicly managed prisons.

Finally, the degree of importation and exportation of prisoners that took place between states with speculative prisons and those in need of additional bed space was extremely high at one point. Why this practice was so prevalent can be traced to many states' overcrowding and fiscal problems; thus, when considering why rural communities sought private prisons, just think about the jobs that are potentially produced as a result of building a prison. According to scholars, a new prison can create anywhere from 200 to 500 permanent jobs. As a result, job-starved communities pushed for prisons as a way to create jobs and to increase their tax base. But if this is the case, why would states export prisoners? Many of the states that exported prisoners found it either cheaper or more convenient to get rid of their problem.

An interesting point about the states that passed legislation prohibiting any private businesses from building speculative prisons is that some of them hoped to win the contracts themselves. They also banned companies from importing prisoners to their states in hopes of acquiring the prisoners at a later date once they entered into the business. North Carolina is one of the states that banned private businesses from building speculative prisons because officials in that state saw prisons as a way to foster economic development in that state. North Carolina has a large rural population, and I suspect they were targeting prisons for economic development because of the problems in their rural communities.

On the other hand, although some states saw how they could benefit from importing and exporting prisoners, others banned the practice and made plans to bring the prisoners home. For instance, "Oregon allowed an existing exportation law to sunset in 2001, effectively banning the export of prisoners. Other states that have exported prisoners are reconsidering their policies: CT, HI, WI, and WY all made plans in 2004 to bring exported prisoners home."[9] Privately managed speculative prisons support my point that privatization is about profits and not efficiency, effectiveness, and quality. Prisoners become commodities as they are traded across borders to those willing to exploit their labor.

ISSUES AND INTERJURISDICTIONAL CONCERNS

According to the author of *Corrections: Past, Present, and Future*, "For-profit speculative prisons raise several troubling issues concerning the three governmental entities involved—the local community, the host state, and the sending state."[10] There are several questions and concerns that should be addressed by the local community regarding for-profit speculative prisons: "What are the economic benefits and costs?; should the private provider be required to reimburse the government for infrastructural enhancements associated the prison's development?; what regulatory control and oversight will local government exercise?; and what is the government liability with regulation in place"?[11]

The first concern for local communities, especially those in rural areas, is the economic benefits presented by for-profit speculative prisons. How many jobs will be created by the speculative prison? The costs to these communities are not weighed as heavily as they should be because the speculative prisons get private financing on the front end; however, once they start getting prisoners, a realistic picture of the costs associated with these prisons can be ascertained. Many of these prisons receive a subsidy, and they also have to be monitored by the correctional agencies in that community. These are additional costs not factored in by local communities when they decide to send prisoners to the speculative prisons. For-profit speculative prisons also establish REITs for the purpose of avoiding tax payments. On top of the subsidy and the formation of the REITs, for-profit speculative prisons become extremely costly to communities, and more often than not they end up being more problematic and costly than the jobs they create. For instance, they have a high number of escapes, they avoid paying taxes by creating REITs, and they treat prisoners with minor health related issues and refer the serious medical problems to a state-funded outside doctor.

The second issue—whether or not the private firm should reimburse the county and/or municipality for governmental costs associated with the prison's development—is, in many instances, a moot question because most speculative prisons are seen as an economic development opportunity for these communities. As a result, the communities pay for many of the infrastructural needs that are necessary to support the building of the prison. Along with providing infrastructural support, many communities provide a subsidy to the for-profit prisons. Again, one can see how communities are encumbered by additional costs to create an economic development opportunity. Later I will discuss the interjurisdictional issues and the potential costs associated with these issues.

A third concern for the local communities is regulatory control and oversight of these for-profit speculative prisons. During the infancy of speculative prisons, communities had very little oversight and regulatory control over these entities. It was not until the speculative prisons began to have problems, such as escapes and misclassification of prisoners, that communities began to pay attention to the need to regulate these prisons. The escapes forced states to look at staffing levels, security issues, and the types of prisoners that were being exported into these prisons. Prisoner escapes and misclassification began to increase the local community's costs because the for-profit speculative prison officials felt that the communities should foot the bill even though the firms frequently understaffed the prisons. Lawsuits and costs began to pile up in these facilities. Seeing the need for regulation and oversight, local officials began to assign monitors to private facilities and write better contracts to govern them.

A final concern for the local communities is whether such regulation—or lack thereof—would increase the local government's liability exposure. This point has been debated extensively, and the main concern is whether or not contracting reduces the government's liability. Although some argue that it does, there are several cases that demonstrate that the government cannot contract away its liability to a private agency; private prisons still must adhere to the Constitution. Additionally, private prisons are considered as "state actors" in civil rights suits, and all relevant constitutional issues must be adhered to whether it is a private or public prison. One advantage that public employees have over their private counterparts is "qualified immunity." This means that private employees are not protected by other immunities the government provides to public employees, such as limitation of monetary damages from prisoners who sue public employees. However, "governments cannot shield themselves entirely from liability by means of contracting, but they can lessen their exposure by doing so."[12] When suits are brought by prisoners in private prisons, "alleging individual rather than systemic group harms, governments will generally not be deemed to have knowledge of the specific acts and injuries, and will not be held responsible."[13] Governments mitigate their liability costs by requiring that "private contractors indemnify them and have relevant public entities named as an insured on the contractor's comprehensive general liability insurance policy."[14]

The point should be stressed that government agencies can contract out their services, but they are not able to remove themselves totally from liability if something happens in the private prison. A 1999 Montana case illustrates this point. A state judge in Montana ruled against the state corrections department's arguments that they were not responsible for prisoners held under contract in a for-profit prison.[15]

Even when private prisons indemnify themselves and the government, neither party is fully protected from liability when things go awry in the prison. For example, "when the District of Columbia signed an $182 million contract with CCA to house prisoners in Youngstown, Ohio, it was told that it was fully indemnified. However, the District of Columbia had to sue CCA to force their compliance with the contract."[16] One of the problems with private agencies indemnifying themselves and the government is that many of them do not follow through with pursing indemnification because of the associated costs. For instance, "in its suit, the District of Columbia claimed CCA refused to indemnify District officials and it failed to obtain the required insurance policy naming the District as insured."[17]

Another fact that government agencies that contract with for-profit speculative prisons must take into consideration is that many for-profit companies may not be able to secure enough liability insurance to protect them from civil suits. Cornell Corrections is a primary example—in a November 18, 1999, SEC filing, the private firm asserted, "we are unable to secure insurance for some unique business risks including riot and civil commotion or the acts of an escaped offender."[18]

Still another example of private agencies having difficulty securing insurance comes from CCA, which was required by Hamilton County, Tennessee, officials to purchase $25 million in insurance to protect the county from liability. Much to the county's chagrin, it was revealed that CCA did not purchase the $25 million insurance policy after the contract was signed. On top of this, CCA informed the county that it could not even get an insurance policy.[19]

Local communities have to be careful when contracting for services from for-profit speculative prisons; the promises of reduced costs are not always met because there are many hidden costs associated with contracting with a for-profit firm. After many painful and expensive lessons, local communities, host states, and sending states have found that the best way to protect themselves from civil suits is to write better contracts governing the exportation, importation, and contracting of prisons.

The host state has another set of problems when it imports prisoners:

- Should the prison be regulated by the local government or the state?

- Who should pay for regulation and oversight?

- Who should handle and pay for emergency situations that arise inside or outside the private prisons?

- Where will prisoners be released after they have served their time?

- How will the prison affect unions?[20]

First, the question of whether the prison should be regulated by the local government or state must be addressed. Based on past problems with private prisons, especially the infamous Youngstown and Brazoria County cases, local governments must get involved with the for-profit firms to help them maintain public safety. Both the local and state governments should have a role in monitoring the operations of these prisons because of past indiscretions. To avoid problems like those in Youngstown, they also should make sure that there are no misclassified prisoners housed in their facilities.

Most public officials feel that local and state governments have a constitutional obligation to provide some oversight and regulation of private facilities. During the initial inception of for-profit speculative prisons, there were very little restrictions, if any, placed on these facilities. It was not until the rampant escapes, beatings, and stabbings that states began to regulate these prisons. During their inception, private prisons not housing in-state prisoners were very problematic because they were not subject to oversight by any state-level agency with any degree of correctional expertise.

The second concern for the host state is who should pay for the oversight of the speculative prisons. This is extremely problematic in cases in which there are no in-state prisoners housed in the prison. Initially, states paid for monitoring these facilities, but many are considering policies that would shift the burden to the private provider by requiring them to pay the monitoring fees regardless of where the prisoner comes from.

A third very sticky problem is who should handle emergency situations that arise inside or outside the private prisons. In addition, who should pay for handling the emergency? Does the local community have the expertise or resources to handle an emergency? All these issues must be worked out in the contract phase before states and local communities contract for services from these speculative prisons. Handling an emergency is another cost many public agencies do not factor into the initial contract. It was only after many of them were burnt by these speculative prisons that better contracts were written to protect themselves from complete liability.

Still another problem for host states is where prisoners should be released after they have served their time. This is an extremely important question considering the number of states that export prisoners. Hawaii has exported prisoners as far away as Texas. With so much distance between prisoners and their families, how do they keep in contact with their families, especially when one factors in the distance and the cost of a collect phone call? Any phone call originating from a prison is a collect phone call, and prison pay phones make about $15,000 a day. Many of the prisoners lose contact with their families, and research shows that prisoners who have no family contact are more likely to reoffend. Speculative prisons that house prisoners from out-of-state are not a good idea in terms of rehabilitation. Most sending states are unwilling to pay for the released prisoner to return home, so these prisoners stay in the communities where they did their time. If states do pay to return released prisoners to their home states, this is another cost not factored into the initial contract that the state has to assume. Having no family and job prospects in the communities where they served their sentences, released prisoners are more likely to reenter the speculative prison that released them. Most critics feel this is the intent of the private prisons—to make sure that prisoners return because incarceration pays. This cycle ends up being costly for the host state because they have to spend money prosecuting these prisoners. If states decide to send criminals to a speculative prison, they pay a per diem for every day the prisoner is incarcerated.

A final concern comes from unions, who have to compete with prison labor that is exploited by for-profit speculative prisons. Prison labor is extremely cheap; as a result, many union workers lose their jobs to prison labor that the for-profit firms contract with corporations to perform a service. Many of the laws banning private prisons have originated from unions, who have lobbied their legislators to ban these prisons because they are directly threatened by prison labor and by the low wages the speculative prisons pay to inmates. Private prisons are not unionized for the most part, and because of this, they attract less qualified employees, which adds to public safety problems.

The sending state also has issues it must take into consideration when exporting prisoners:

- Does the department have statutory authority to place prisoners out of state?

- Are there minimum qualifications that the private provider must meet?

- Is there a mechanism to monitor the contract to ensure that requirements are being met?

- What is the sending state's liability exposure?

- How will prisoners be transported to the private facility?

- How will the effectiveness of privatization be assessed?[21]

With each of these issues, there are costs that the host state, local community, and sending state must address before the prisoners are exported or imported. Although there is a belief that governments are relieved of many of the responsibilities and costs associated with managing a prison, this is far from the truth; because of poorly written contracts, states have had to ask many of the questions in this section as a means to protect themselves from civil suits and opportunistic speculative prison providers.

Summary

Speculative prisons are accompanied by numerous concerns for the host state. During the beginning of the speculative prison building, many states were not as savvy as they are now. Today, host states do a better job managing the interjurisdictional issues that arise as a result of exportation and importation of prisoners. However, as a result of their past inexperience in dealing with for-profit speculative prisons, many of the local communities, sending states, and hosts states were exploited by the private providers. How so? The speculative prisons avoided paying additional expenses above the contract because they knew that they could not manage the prison for the agreed upon amount when they submitted their initial bid.

Private prisons have become an integral part of many communities across the country, in particular for their economies. Private prisons generate jobs for the residents of these communities and concomitantly increase their tax base. As a result, even though prisons run by private entities may not always be cost-effective, states are willing to privatize. In some cases, to get rid of the prison would destroy the community's economy. States' hesitance to be tougher on these prisons is understandable, but it does not excuse the states' obligation to the prisoners who have been commodified in the process. Private prison officials are extremely powerful and highly connected, and the only way for states and local communities to regulate them is to write better contracts to protect themselves.

Chapter Five

Private Prisons: A Vested Interest to Incarcerate

Introduction

Advocates of privatization and for-profit providers of prisons contend that because they can manage prisons better than the public, prisons should be turned over to the private sector to manage. Critics are quick to point out that there are no definitive studies to support the claims of private firms that they can deliver better services than the public. What is clear is that profit is the primary reason for-profit prisons operate. This chapter looks at the economic incentives that underlie prison privatization:

- The political economy of prisons
- Public trading of private prison stock
- The exploitation of prison labor
- Prisons used as an economic development tool
- Campaign financing and lobbying used to influence legislation
- The attendant corrections-commercial complex that has developed with the prison industry

The chapter examines the transfer of dollars from urban centers to rural centers when prisoners are exported and the impact this has on the urban centers. It also explores the impact of felony disenfranchisement on these prisoners and the deprivement of educational opportunities once prisoners are incarcerated and after their release. Critics contend that these strategies are used to fuel the growth of the prison industrial complex, citing the billion dollar industry that private prisons have become as proof of their claims that the industry is profit driven.

Critics ask a series of questions to reinforce their argument that for-profit prisons are being legitimized in a way that disregards the nonprofit aspects of the prison sector. For instance, why else would for-profit providers give millions of dollars to legislators responsible for making laws that benefit their industry? Why do for-profit prisons' CEOs serve on the ALEC Criminal Justice Task Force committee along with the same legislators to whom they make campaign contributions? Why do for-profit providers of prisons donate money to ALEC? Critics contend that the answer to these questions is that for-profit prisons have a vested interest to incarcerate, and these strategies help them meet the annual profit goals they have promised their stockholders.

Another salient point explored in this chapter is that private prisons stock is publicly traded. Even the novice investor understands the goal of the stock market. Because their stock is publicly traded, they must have a vested interest to incarcerate, critics contend. If the goal is to maximize shareholder wealth, how is that accomplished? The answer is that you accomplish this by lobbying for laws favorable to your industry, which for-profit providers are very successful at doing. In light of the fact that there is a vested interest to incarcerate, should a state give up to a private entity the responsibility to punish, especially to an industry that benefits from punishment? Because private prisons trade on the stock exchange, are they more interested in profits than rehabilitation? Considering that private providers lobby for stiffer sentences and other punitive laws to incapacitate prisoners longer, it would seem that they are more interested in profits. This chapter attempts to answer many of the important questions that demonstrate the conflict of interest that exists when prisons become private.

Finally, it is obvious that any for-profit organization is interested in maximizing their profits, and for-profit prisons are not an exception. That is not really the issue of this chapter; the issue here is that the profit motive interferes with the democratic process in this case and is detrimental to society in ways not just harmful to prisoners. Currently, the way for-profit firms achieve their goals through ALEC negatively impacts the political process because it circumvents and skews the process of check and balances. Additionally, it feeds the distrust that citizens have felt toward their government over the last thirty years.

The Political Economy of Prison Privatization

The privatization of prisons has been politicized beyond comprehension. The private sector and the public sector are so intertwined that it would take years to unravel the relationship that exists within this industry. This intertwining is extremely obvious in rural communities, which at one time would have sued to stop a prison from locating in their community. Now rural communities ask their legislators to pursue private prisons because their livelihood depends on them. Legislators oblige by passing laws drafted in ALEC's Criminal Justice Task Force Committee and returning home to write bills based on the legislation crafted in this committee. The punitiveness of laws suggested by ALEC accomplishes three objectives: it guarantees prisoners to the for-profit prison providers, it guarantees that rural residents keep their jobs, and it guarantees the legislators a certain degree of job security and campaign contributions.

According to the text Theories of Political Economy, "it is often assumed that political economy involves an integration of politics and economics."[1] In the case of private prisons, should this integration of politics and economics intersect despite the fact that the power to punish is being commodified? How else do you explain the fact that the imprisonment rate has increased by almost 500 percent within the last twenty years?[2] I pose this question because the crime rate, relatively speaking, is going down; this begs the question, why is the imprisonment rate going up? Critics contend that the politicization of crime—aided by the tendency of the media to sensationalize crime

109

and the contributions for-profit prisons make to politicians who run on "get tough on crime" campaigns—feeds the prison industrial complex. This campaign disproportionately benefits rural communities at the expense of minority communities: dollars are transferred from urban centers to rural communities because of the way the census counts prisoners.

Overall, people are extremely misinformed about the political-economic benefits of building a prison in a rural community. In some cases, the prison industry has taken priority over educational spending. There is a lot of money being made from this industry, and the public schools are mostly attended by the poor; as a result, schools are no longer a priority. Many of these same students who are being shortchanged end up in these private prisons as a result of this social exclusion. According to the South West Regional Assembly, social exclusion occurs "when an individual is prevented from participating in any of the key economic, social and political activities, in the society in which they live."[3] To get an idea of the benefits of constructing and maintaining a prison, let's examine the following numbers:

- Over $80 billion—a sum larger than annual budgets of most nations in the world—is spent annually by the United States on prisons.[4]

- In the last ten years in California, twenty prisons were built versus one state university campus and one university of California campus; 26,000 jobs were added to various state corrections departments. The Department of Corrections operating budget increased by 14 percent versus the whole state budget, which only increased by 7 percent. In 1985 there were 7,570 prison guards; in 1990 there were 14,249; and in 1994 there were 25,547.[5]

- Since 1994, the year in which a special session of the state legislature was called to address the problem of prison overcrowding, it was estimated that, through the year 2002, the state Department of Corrections of California would spend 62 percent of its capital budget ($45,334,671) on new and expanded private prisons. Each of their new prisons comes saddled with new operating costs, which contribute to a continued rerouting of taxpayer dollars from education to incarceration.[6]

- Mississippi built sixteen new correctional facilities, including six for-profit prisons, in the 1990s. The state has built no new four-year colleges or universities in over fifty years.[7]

- Between 1989 and 1998, Mississippi saw per capita state corrections appropriations rise by 115 percent, while per-capita state higher education appropriations increased by less than 1 percent.[8]

- There are almost twice as many African American men in Mississippi in prison (13,837) as in colleges and universities (7,330). The state spends more per year to incarcerate a prisoner ($10,672) than to send them to college ($6,871).[9]

The for-profit prisons have transformed into a vast industrial system at the expense of education in many states. The police, lawyers, court staff, lobbyists, convicts, long-distance phone service providers, and prison personnel all are a part of this growing business behemoth that generates billions of dollars for the for-profit prisons. The lobbyists for for-profit prisons are so effective at generating profits that, at one point, they asked the state of Mississippi to pay millions of dollars for "ghost prisoners;" Mississippi had no prisoners to send the for-profit prison, but they still had a contractual obligation to pay even though no prisoners were housed in the facility. Reporters coined the phrase "ghost prisoners" to refer to this arrangement. The state agreed to pay for "ghost prisoners" until 2001 because of severe fiscal problems.[10] Despite the decade-long decline in the crime rate during the time, the for-profit provider asked the state to pay for prisoners that were not in the facility; in addition, many states were still engaged in a frenzy of prison construction and expansion, which led to twenty-seven states being over capacity by at least 1 percent.[11] This data suggests that for-profit providers effectively grew their market despite the fact that the crime rate declined over a ten-year period. How were they able to continue to build prisons and reach overcapacity in their prisons? They imported prisoners, lobbied for reduction of probation and parole, and lobbied for probation and parole officers to be more strict, which meant that many prisoners were sent back to jail for technical violations of their probation and parole. These strategies employed by for-profit prisons are definitely geared toward increasing profits. In effect, "in the prisons business, where a quarter of a century ago the stakeholders were principally public officials and employees, prisoners, and a nebulous sense of public interest, the stakeholders today include these but also voters; labor unions; private for-profit corporations; communities housing prisons; and politicians, lobbyists, and political organizations that represent all these interests."[12]

Private Prisons and the Stock Market

As the for-profit prisons have grown, they have made their mark on the economy. The industry leveled off and went through a downturn but appears to be picking up contracts at the federal level. Investors have paid attention to this growth: "a March 1996 research document from Equitable Securities in Nashville describes the prison industry as 'very attractive' and issues 'strong buy' advice to investors."[13] This statement captures the feelings about the existing private prison industry as privatization of prisons at the federal level has started to increase; the language used demonstrates that the prison industry is profit-driven. As a matter of fact, the Paine Webber Group is the prime stockholder of CCA, the leading for-profit prison provider.[14] For many; the idea that prisons generate a profit is not problematic because prisoners should pay while incarcerated. However, that is not the issue; the issue is that a function that many deem inherently public is being assigned to an entity that benefits financially from punishment. Private prisons are using the stock market to generate these profits, and most of the companies are being underwritten by well-established Wall Street investment firms. In essence, they have commodified the prisoners. Should the state allow such a thing to happen? The Constitution provides that the states have to protect the general welfare of its citizens; although certain rights are surrendered upon incarceration, the Constitution does not make exceptions as it concerns the commodification of citizens. Experts figure that, in order for a private prison to be profitable, it must be filled between 90 and 95 percent capacity, and most private prisons are over capacity by 1 percent. Prisoners mean profits, and the surest way to guarantee profits is to lobby for stiffer sentences. For-profit providers have been vigilant and unashamed in lobbying for more punitive laws. For them, more laws mean more dollars.

Sadly, since the 1980s, "fewer citizens realize that private corporations—whose stocks are the object of investment by an estimated 69 million people or approximately 44 percent of all American household—have begun to assume the responsibility for housing these exploding numbers of prisoners."[15] How so? Well, many of us invest in the crime control industry through our 401(k) plans, which purchase stock from the more than 2,000 mutual funds in operation, and these derive at least some of their profits from prisoner labor or prison construction.[16] College graduates may be tied to the prison industry through the Sodexho Alliance, Sodexho Marriott Services, the food service arm of the organization that holds contracts for food services in private prisons and in some colleges and universities. If you ever had a meal plan or dined in the cafeteria while attending or visiting a college, you may have unknowingly contributed to growing the prison industrial complex and the exploitation of prisoners. The hotel chain Sodexho Marriott was also tied to the prison industry through its food service division. If you have stayed at a Marriott hotel or have eaten food there, you may have been involved in the prison industry.

The government has sat idly by as for-profit prisons continue to publicly trade their stock. At the apex of its success in the 1990s, CCA moved from the NASDAQ to the New York Stock Exchange. Additionally, CCA, the industry leader with the largest market share, was the first company to trade on the stock exchange when it went public in 1993, nine years after in entered into the for-profit prison industry. Their stock was considered to be *the* stock to buy in the 1990s. According to industry analysts in the 1990s, prospects for

113

future growth in the for-profit prison industry looked bright. This projection proved to be true for many years until the bottom fell out, and private prison stocks dropped precipitously after several high-profile incidents, which created a backlash against private prisons. Their stock prices have rebounded and stabilized, and the increasing use of for-profit prisons by the federal government may send stocks soaring again. Considering the USA PATRIOT Act I and II, the Intelligence Reform and Terrorism Prevention Act of 2004, the fiscal condition of states, and the continued problem of prison overcrowding, the crackdown on immigration may prove to be just what the doctor ordered for private prison stock. As it concerns for-profit prison providers, there does appear to be some teeth to the idea that the current climate of terrorism and law and order has helped CCA and the Geo Group Inc. (formerly Wackenhut); however, the Cornell Companies has not fared as well, although they are projected to be the company with the most upside.

Now, should an organization that benefits from punishment and clearly is interested in maximizing its stock be able to continue in this business? There is nothing wrong with this picture for many people, but the problem is that these organizations lobby for laws that incapacitate prisoners for longer periods of time to ensure they have prisoners from which to extract free labor. Prison labor generates the bulk of their profits, which, in turn, makes them more appealing to potential investors. The prisoners help private prisons compete for contracts from IBM, Dell, and other Fortune 500 companies, but those prisoners are paid slave wages. It is a stretch to believe that for-profit prisons are in the business because they can do it better than the government, as they would have the public believe. They are in this industry because there are billions of dollars being made from inmate labor.

CCA was not the only company to go public:

- Cornell Corrections (formerly Cornell Cox) began trading on the American Stock Exchange in October 1996 with an initial public offering underwritten by Dillon and Read & Co., Equitable Securities and ING Barings, which raised $37 million.[17]

- Wackenhut Corrections went public in July 1994 with a $17 per share initial offering underwritten by Prudential Securities.[18]

- Avalon Enterprises (now Avalon Correctional Services) entered into the public arena of the stock market in 1991.

- Correctional Services Corp. (formerly Esmor Correctional Services Inc.) began trading with an initial $5.2 million public offering underwritten by Jane Montgomery Scott—a subsidiary of Penn Mutual Life Insurance.[19]

To get an idea of their profitability, it is necessary to explore the history of ten of the for-profit prisons: Avalon Correctional Services Inc., Cornell Companies Inc., Correctional Services Corporation, CCA, and the Geo Group Inc. (formerly Wackenhut). All continue to trade on the stock exchanges according to their 2003 annual reports: Avalon's 2003 revenues were $25.3 million; Cornell's were $271.6 million; Correctional Services' were $135.8 million; CCA's were a little over $1 billion; and Geo Group's were $617.5 million. CCA is clearly the leader in the profitability arena; they also have the most for-profit prisons. CiviGenics Inc., Maranatha Corrections, LLC, and Tuscolameta Inc. do not publish information on whether or not they have ever traded on the stock exchange. They disclose very little information about their business dealings. Dominion Correctional Services, LLC, is now managed by Cornell Companies, and Management and Training Corporation does not provide information on their Web site regarding whether or not they are publicly held.

On another note, one of the interesting factors that jumps out at the keen reader is that several of the for-profit companies have undergone name changes. Many of them changed their names after various high-profile incidents that cast a negative light on managing prisons for profit. The strategy has worked for many of them because they are still in the business, while others have dropped out of the industry or have been bought out by either CCA or the Geo Group Inc. A few for-profit providers have been very successful in surviving fiascos such as prisoner beatings and escapes. The ones that have survived have been able to grow their market share of the prison industry via acquisition and lobbying for laws that are favorable to their industry. It helps that many of them are highly connected. CCA's chairman emeritus, Thomas Beasley, who cofounded the company in 1983, previously served as the chairman of the Tennessee Republican Party. George Wackenhut, an ex-FBI agent and founder of Wackenhut Corporation (the Geo Group Inc.), and Mike Quinlan, senior vice president of CCA and former employee of the Federal Bureau of Prisons, were also high-level officials in the government at one time. These men are able to take their concerns directly to state and national leaders because of their former government positions. As a result of their contacts, these corporations have been able to maintain their market share in many cases, especially in the southern part of the United States, despite the high-profile incidents that have plagued them since their inception. It also helps that the people involved are prisoners, and very few people with power speak for them.

By virtue of publicly trading their stocks, the classical arguments for prison privatization fall by the wayside. Why? Because the idea that private prison stock is traded on the stock exchange begs the question: should the government give up the power to punish to an entity that benefits from punishment, especially one that makes billions of dollars from punishment?

Prison Labor

Some have asserted, based on the disproportionate number of blacks that are incarcerated, that prison privatization in the United States is an extension of Jim Crow laws. Under Jim Crow, African Americans were deprived of their life, liberty, and chance of happiness. Additionally, blacks had no rights to sell their labor. After emancipation, blacks began to compete in the labor market with whites; as a result, employment opportunities diminished for whites in the same socioeconomic class as the newly manumitted blacks. When employment opportunities started to diminish for poor whites, they began to devise ways to circumvent the newly acquired rights of blacks and to recapture their source of cheap—or better yet, free—labor. Leaders in these communities began to target certain crimes that blacks were most likely to commit, such as vagrancy, in order to imprison blacks for the purpose of reclaiming the cheap labor convicts provided. The convict lease system was devised under this new system of slavery— imprisonment. Convicts were leased out to private agencies and the state was paid their wages for the work they performed. As private prisons have grown, so has the use of prison labor. Is there a connection between increased prison labor and privatization? There is evidence to suggest that this is the case. Why is this a problem? For many critics the problem is the economic incentives that are gained by private prisons who exploit prisoner labor.

Moreover, African American men are being incarcerated at a rate approximately four times the incarceration rate of black South African men under apartheid. As a result of this increased incarceration of black men, the United States has "managed to replicate—at least on a statistical level—the shame of chattel slavery in this country."[20] As a matter of fact, African Americans have become the numerical majority in prisons, and this is a first. The war on drugs, along with the lobbying done by ALEC on the behalf of for-profit prisons, is the culprit of this perverse statistic. Table 5.1 reinforces the point that imprisonment is the new form of slavery.

These findings demonstrate that it is now prisons that deprive black men of their rights in the United States. The biggest reason for an increase in the incarceration of African American males is the war on drugs, which has been characterized as the new Jim Crow and, critics contend, a strategy to capture free labor. Additionally, the war on drugs has "circumvented rights such as the Fourth Amendment for African American males,"[21] especially by allowing more discretion as police have stepped up "pretextual stops," in which cars are pulled over or searches are conducted under false pretenses. The U.S. Supreme Court has aided the efforts of the police by upholding convictions based on pretextual stops, a practice which has further eroded the Fourth Amendment rights of African American males in particular. This practice has also led to the Constitutional degradation of African American males in the area of suffrage because, once convicted or while pleading out a case, many African American males permanently lose the right to vote in about ten states. Additionally,

Table 5.1
Projected Black Inmate Population and Black Male Slaves

Year	Projected black male inmate population	Year	Black male slave population
2000	792,000	1820	783,781
2005	1,040,027	1830	1,001,986
2008	1,224,719	1840	1,244,000
2017	1,999,916	1860	1,981,395

Note: Boyd derives the data on the number of African American male inmates from the baseline of two million prisoners and the fact that African-American men represent 41.3% of the total inmate population. He assumes a constant yearly growth rate of 5.6% for the prison population, which was the average rate of growth for the decade from 1990 to 2000 Boyd uses to compute the future growth rate of African American inmates. He compiles the data on slavery from the Inter-University Consortium for Political and Social Research, Study 00003, Historical Demographics, Economic, and Social Data: U.S., 1790-1970 (Ann Arbor: ICPSR). Remaining data from the U.S. Department of Justice, Bureau of Justice Statistics, Prisoners and Jail Inmates at Midyear 2000 (Washington, DC: U.S. Department of Justice, March 2001).

Source: Graham Boyd, "The Drug War Is the New Jim Crow," NACLA Report on the Americas, July/August 2001.

prisons have managed to replicate the erosion of Constitutional rights of the Jim Crow system by disproportionately incarcerating and targeting black males for incarceration and cheap labor. The literacy tests, poll taxes, and felony disenfranchisement of Jim Crow parallel today's harmful practices of depriving drug offenders of financial aid, the right to vote, the opportunity to achieve gainful employment after release. A question that should be addressed is whether private prisons devise schemes to recapture prisoner labor because the bulk of their profits is generated by prisoners. Additionally, although their disproportionate incarceration indicates minorities are targeted by the criminal justice industry, all poor people are caught up in the imprisonment tide to acquire cheap labor. The discussion about African Americans is underscored because prisons have always been a means of social control for blacks. With poor schools and diminishing opportunities, minorities are an easy target for the prison entrepreneurs who lobby for stiffer laws to ensnare the poor, who are more likely to commit crimes.

The term "prisoner" refers to those in the physical custody of a state or federal adult correctional agency.[22] According to the latest data from the Bureau of Justice Statistics, more than 2 million people are incarcerated. Private prisons held about 6.5 percent of state and federal prisons in 2003.[23] That amounts to 94,361 prisoners to provide convict labor to for-profit prisons in 2003.[24]

It should be noted that there are six different systems that have been important at one time or another during the historical prison labor controversy:[25]

1. Under the *contract system,* an individual or firm would contract with the state for prisoners and negotiate the amount per day to be paid per prisoner laborer.

2. The *piece-price system* is basically the same arrangement as the contract system, except the contractor pays the state an agreed price per unit of product rather than per unit of labor.[26]

3. Under the *lease system,* a contractor is paid by the state to feed, clothe, house, and guard the prisoners and to pay the state a stipulated amount per man per day.[27]

4. The *state-account system* functions as a manufacturing business and disposes of the product on the open market.[28]

5. The *state-use system* is designed as such where the state conducts a business of manufacture or other production, but the use or sale of the product is limited to the same institution or another state or federal institution or department;[29] and

6. The *public works and ways system* used prison labor for the construction and repair of prison and other public buildings, roads, parks, and bridges, as well as for flood control, reforestation, and land clearance. Prisoners did not produce goods.[30]

PRISON INDUSTRIES IN AMERICAN CORRECTIONS

The impetus behind the need for prison labor has been the prison industries that have developed around the corrections industry. These industries continue to be viewed negatively by unions, who directly compete with prison labor in many sectors. Labor unions view the prison industries as unfair competition, and there is some truth to their fears.

According to those who manage them, prison industries' primary goals are to eliminate prisoner idleness and to provide prisoners with a skill. However, critics contend that it is a perverse way to exploit labor for personal gain. It appears that Congress accepts the former argument; it has passed several acts supported by the executive branch to remove some restrictions on interstate commerce of prison-made goods. Congress agrees with the idea that prisoners should work during their tenure in prison.

In 1984, the Prison Industries Enhancement Act was amended and became the Justice Assistance Act, which exempted prison industries from federal restraints and encouraged private sector involvement. President Jimmy Carter promptly signed this act, demonstrating his support for the idea that prisoners should be employed while in prison. The acts resulted in the certification of twenty-three pilot prison programs working in a partnership with the private sector. These projects stipulated that a portion of prisoner wages must go to programs that aid crime victims, and representatives of organized labor and private industry must be consulted when prisoner work programs are established. The acts also required that prison workers be paid commensurate with those in the private sector; that state labor officials must certify that private-sector workers will not be displaced or existing labor contracts infringed upon; and that prisoners must participate voluntarily and receive standard benefits.[31] Although work in prison is purportedly voluntary, if they do not volunteer to work, many prisoners cannot receive good time credits, which reduce their prison time. This is problematic because many of the for-profit prisons benefit from prisoners refusing to work because that means more time in prison and guaranteed per diems for each day the prisoners are incarcerated.

. Many of them have worked
·arcerated and have the skills
ley are discriminated against
. However, a *New York Times*
are far more likely to find
two Princeton professor who
ite men with prison records
i jobs in New York City than
ire offered jobs just as often—
have never been arrested."[45]
if you cannot use them once
>rity? UNICOR and for-profit
when they foster the use of
because they know that many
:ause of the felony conviction.
on successfully back into soci-
nade by the Fortune 500 com-
:arceration and the for-profit
· question is this: should pris-
Standards Act (FLSA), which
pay, recordkeeping, and child
: and part-time workers?
>risoners in the public and pri-
lis is a critical policy question

>ns are the worst exploiters of
·un prison industries are the
n labor system despite healthy
s, this question appears to be
it is not likely to punish itself

: Development

aware of the impact of dein-
ave been very effective in per-
.egislators to allow prisons in

The contemporary federal perspective opened the door for the present models of prison industries. This rebirth is predicated on building an alliance with private enterprise while assuaging the fears of organized labor; they have been unable to accomplish the latter. A business-like approach to the operation of prison industries and the development of industrial models is reflected in this trend.[32]

CONTEMPORARY MODELS

The strength of the relationship between the private sector and the correctional institution differs depending on the prison industry model. Each model has strengths and weaknesses. In the *government-use model*, prison industries limit the sale of their manufactured goods to state and local government markets. Any participation by the private sector is minimal in this model. *Government-use* programs are financed through appropriations from correctional budgets, which in some states means less money for education. Allegedly, revenues/profits are redistributed to those budgets from which they were drawn. Prisoners are paid very little for their labor under this arrangement.

The government-use model maintains control within the public sphere; "therefore, it can more easily accommodate correctional goals, that is, maximizing prisoner employment and reducing idleness."[33] Public risks and fiscal rewards are minimal for the state, although the market is limited in this model. The *government-use model* is the most prevalent form of prison industry arrangement in the contemporary correctional setting. States such as Illinois, Maryland, and Louisiana are excellent examples of this model.

The *joint-venture model* entails contracting with private sector businesses such as IBM, Dell, Lee Jeans, Boeing, Victoria's Secret, and Eddie Bauer.[34] The *joint-venture model* accords opportunities for production of private firm products and the chance to purchase prison-produced products. Transactions between the public and private prison are jointly managed, but "the correctional agency is typically in charge of organizational structure, industry goals, wage scales, and prisoner hiring."[35] Product design, production, marketing, and distribution are handled by the private sector. Corcraft's involvement with

121

the New York State Correctional Services as their priso
ing division is an example of a joint-venture project.[36]

The *corporate model* has the look of a private sector
emphasis in this model is on security, fostering maxi
involvement, and providing work opportunities
Correctional influence decreases in this model when
with the private sector. Correctional agency goals ma
ondary to profitability, which has been the case in
prison sector.

The *corporate model* has been utilized in several s
Prison and Rehabilitative Industries and Diversifi
(PRIDE), a nonprofit entity created by the Florida le
excellent example of this model. Another example
Prison Industries (commonly referred to as FPI or by
UNICOR),[37] "a wholly government-owned corporati
by Congress on June 23, 1934."[38] Its mission since 19
provide job skills for prisoners confined within the Fed
Prisons. In the 1996 federal fiscal year, FPI sales were
and they employed 17,379 prisoners—by far the large
trial program in the nation, although California and T
prisoners in their systems.[39] It is understandable why
ons engage in exploitation of prison labor because t
has done so since 1934. To top it off, FPI is statutor
selling its wares to the federal government, and the
Defense accounts for 60 percent of FPI sales.[40] Other
include the General Services Administration, the H
of Prisons, the Social Security Administration, the
Justice, the U.S. Postal Service, the Department of Trar
Department of the Treasury, the Department of A
the Department of Veterans Affairs.[41]

The *free-enterprise model* is the most independent a
the prison industry. Decisions are made by the priva
sively, which minimizes public sector risk. Prisoner
room and board under this model. The telephone res
which is operated by Best Western International insid
Arizona Correctional Institute for Women, and Zephy

release because of their prison record
years for these corporations while in
and experience to do the job, but
because of their past criminal record
report showed that white parolees
employment than black parolees. The
authored this study found that "W
receive far more offers for entry-lev
black men with identical records, and
if not more so—than black men who
Why acquire skills while incarcerated
released, especially if you are a min
providers of prisons are disingenuou
prison labor to develop prisoner's skills
will not be employable after release be
In the future, if prisoners are to transi
ety, some kind of concession has to be
panies that hire prisoners during in
providers who contract them out. Th
oners be covered by the Fair Labor
establishes minimum wage, overtime
labor standards affecting full-tim
Considering the degree of exploitation
vate prison industries are subject to,
that must be addressed.

A misperception is that private pris
prisoner labor. In fact, government-
worst because they dominate the priso
gains by private prison industries; th
more complex because the governme
for exploitation of prisoner labor.

Private Prisons as Economi

For-profit providers of prisons, being
dustrialization on rural communities,
suading rural communities and their

The contemporary federal perspective opened the door for the present models of prison industries. This rebirth is predicated on building an alliance with private enterprise while assuaging the fears of organized labor; they have been unable to accomplish the latter. A business-like approach to the operation of prison industries and the development of industrial models is reflected in this trend.[32]

CONTEMPORARY MODELS

The strength of the relationship between the private sector and the correctional institution differs depending on the prison industry model. Each model has strengths and weaknesses. In the *government-use model*, prison industries limit the sale of their manufactured goods to state and local government markets. Any participation by the private sector is minimal in this model. *Government-use* programs are financed through appropriations from correctional budgets, which in some states means less money for education. Allegedly, revenues/profits are redistributed to those budgets from which they were drawn. Prisoners are paid very little for their labor under this arrangement.

The government-use model maintains control within the public sphere; "therefore, it can more easily accommodate correctional goals, that is, maximizing prisoner employment and reducing idleness."[33] Public risks and fiscal rewards are minimal for the state, although the market is limited in this model. The *government-use model* is the most prevalent form of prison industry arrangement in the contemporary correctional setting. States such as Illinois, Maryland, and Louisiana are excellent examples of this model.

The *joint-venture model* entails contracting with private sector businesses such as IBM, Dell, Lee Jeans, Boeing, Victoria's Secret, and Eddie Bauer.[34] The *joint-venture model* accords opportunities for production of private firm products and the chance to purchase prison-produced products. Transactions between the public and private prison are jointly managed, but "the correctional agency is typically in charge of organizational structure, industry goals, wage scales, and prisoner hiring."[35] Product design, production, marketing, and distribution are handled by the private sector. Corcraft's involvement with

121

the New York State Correctional Services as their prison manufacturing division is an example of a joint-venture project.[36]

The *corporate model* has the look of a private sector business. The emphasis in this model is on security, fostering maximum prisoner involvement, and providing work opportunities for prisoners. Correctional influence decreases in this model when control resides with the private sector. Correctional agency goals may become secondary to profitability, which has been the case in the for-profit prison sector.

The *corporate model* has been utilized in several states. Florida's Prison and Rehabilitative Industries and Diversified Enterprises (PRIDE), a nonprofit entity created by the Florida legislature, is an excellent example of this model. Another example is the Federal Prison Industries (commonly referred to as FPI or by its trade name, UNICOR),[37] "a wholly government-owned corporation established by Congress on June 23, 1934."[38] Its mission since 1934 has been to provide job skills for prisoners confined within the Federal Bureau of Prisons. In the 1996 federal fiscal year, FPI sales were $495.4 million, and they employed 17,379 prisoners—by far the largest prison industrial program in the nation, although California and Texas hold more prisoners in their systems.[39] It is understandable why for-profit prisons engage in exploitation of prison labor because the government has done so since 1934. To top it off, FPI is statutorily restricted to selling its wares to the federal government, and the Department of Defense accounts for 60 percent of FPI sales.[40] Other key customers include the General Services Administration, the Federal Bureau of Prisons, the Social Security Administration, the Department of Justice, the U.S. Postal Service, the Department of Transportation, the Department of the Treasury, the Department of Agriculture, and the Department of Veterans Affairs.[41]

The *free-enterprise model* is the most independent arrangement in the prison industry. Decisions are made by the private sector exclusively, which minimizes public sector risk. Prisoners pay for their room and board under this model. The telephone reservation center, which is operated by Best Western International inside the (Phoenix) Arizona Correctional Institute for Women, and Zephyr Products Inc., which operates a manufacturing facility just outside the Lansing, Kansas, correctional facility, are examples of this model.

This symbiotic relationship between the public sector and private prisons involves the dependence of private capital on the state. In other words, it involves the use of the state's coercive instrumentalities and traditional jurisdiction over captive or dependent subpopulations as a means of mobilizing cheap labor for private entrepreneurs.[42] Similar to the early nineteenth century institutions of confinement, today's prisons are a critical source of revenue for states. Contemporary prisoners are counted among the limited sources of revenue at the state's disposal. As penal institutions became centers of production, prison labor became viewed more as a means of enforcing discipline.[43] Institutions of confinement became both a way to broaden state fiscal base and a means whereby private owners accumulated capital and secured disciplined labor. These purposes were mutually reinforcing.[44]

Finally, as prisoners continue to work for little or no wages, many critics compare their work environments to "sweat shops." Prison labor is comparable to Third World labor. In fact, prison labor is so competitive with Third World labor, many corporations are using prison labor instead of taking advantage of the cheap labor abroad. Although some prisoners make minimum wage, many only see 50 cents after various deductions are taken out of their check for room and board and victim restitution; in contrast, for-profit prison corporations make off with millions of dollars. This raises questions of social equity. Because the purpose of any corporation is to generate profits, punitive laws bode well for private prison providers; therefore, it is in their interest to lobby for tougher laws to capture cheap labor, and minorities have been intentionally targeted and disproportionately impacted by these laws. Scholars characterize the war on drugs as the new Jim Crow because of the number of blacks in prison compared to the percentage of the population they comprise, as well as the pernicious impact it has on African American men.

Another unfortunate aspect of prison labor is that, while prisoners work for Chevron, IBM, Motorola, Compaq, Texas Instruments, Honeywell, Microsoft, Victoria Secret, and Boeing while incarcerated, many cannot secure employment with these employers upon their release because of their prison records. Many of them have worked years for these corporations while incarcerated and have the skills and experience to do the job, but they are discriminated against because of their past criminal records. However, a *New York Times* report showed that white parolees are far more likely to find employment than black parolees. The two Princeton professor who authored this study found that "White men with prison records receive far more offers for entry-level jobs in New York City than black men with identical records, and are offered jobs just as often—if not more so—than black men who have never been arrested."[45] Why acquire skills while incarcerated if you cannot use them once released, especially if you are a minority? UNICOR and for-profit providers of prisons are disingenuous when they foster the use of prison labor to develop prisoner's skills because they know that many will not be employable after release because of the felony conviction. In the future, if prisoners are to transition successfully back into society, some kind of concession has to be made by the Fortune 500 companies that hire prisoners during incarceration and the for-profit providers who contract them out. The question is this: should prisoners be covered by the Fair Labor Standards Act (FLSA), which establishes minimum wage, overtime pay, recordkeeping, and child labor standards affecting full-time and part-time workers? Considering the degree of exploitation prisoners in the public and private prison industries are subject to, this is a critical policy question that must be addressed.

A misperception is that private prisons are the worst exploiters of prisoner labor. In fact, government-run prison industries are the worst because they dominate the prison labor system despite healthy gains by private prison industries; thus, this question appears to be more complex because the government is not likely to punish itself for exploitation of prisoner labor.

Private Prisons as Economic Development

For-profit providers of prisons, being aware of the impact of deindustrialization on rural communities, have been very effective in persuading rural communities and their legislators to allow prisons in their communities. Even state budget woes due to poor planning, terrorism, a weakening economy, and globalization have not stopped states from spending exorbitant amounts of taxpayer money on economic development subsidies to private prisons, according to the report entitled *Jail Breaks: Economic Development Subsidies to Private Prisons*. The study by Good Jobs First, a nonprofit group that helps ensure that economic development subsidies are effective and accountable, found that for-profit privately built and managed prisons have received subsidies, such as tax-advantaged financing, property tax reductions, infrastructure assistance, and training grants/tax credits. Their study, which examined sixty prisons located in nineteen states, found the following:

> 73 percent, of the facilities received one or more development subsidies; $628 million in tax-free bonds and other government-issued securities were used to finance 37 percent of the prisons studied; 38 percent received property tax abatements or other tax reductions; 23 percent received an infrastructure subsidy; 37 percent of the facilities received low-cost construction financing through tax-free bonds or other government-issued debt securities; of the nineteen states, facilities in at least seventeen were found to have received subsidies; and the "big two" Corrections Corporation of America and Wackenhut Corrections Corporation were extensively subsidized.[46]

Although the states subsidize the for-profit prisons, in some instances it does not ensure their success because private prisons need prisoners. With the crime rate trending downward in many areas, private prisons have had to come up with ways to keep profits up. To support their profit maximization efforts, they have solicited prisoners from other states to ensure that prisons remain full. Not only do they subsidize these prisons but they also facilitate the exportation of prisoners from other states by not regulating them as much as they should given the fact that prisons are not the same as regular corporations.

Essentially, exportation of prisoners has become a strategy for for-profit prisons and legislators to ensure that the prison can sustain the community. Prisoners mean jobs to these communities, so subsidies help keep the for-profit prisons in those communities, and their legislators draft laws for passage through the ALEC Criminal Justice Task Force Committee for the purpose of incapacitating prisoners for longer periods of time. As a result, the prison is a part of rural community's economic development strategy to revitalize the area.

Studies have shown that neither prisons nor stadiums live up to their initial promise of projected economic development profits. Most studies assessing the positive financial impact of prisons on communities lack methodological rigor; thus, the findings are questionable. This alone should prompt states to be guarded regarding building a prison in their community to spur economic growth. However, this has not deterred communities from building prisons. As a matter of fact, Appleton, Minnesota, and Hinton, Oklahoma, were among the first towns to take matters into their own hands by building and operating prisons for economic development in the early 1990s.[47] Additionally, the buildup of prisons in rural communities for economic purposes does not stop with these two prisons because "today, 57 percent of U.S. prisons are in rural areas."[48]

Based on the number of prisons built, these findings that prisons do not necessarily grow the economy have not been a deterrent because prisons are a growth industry. Consequently, they depend upon an ever-increasing number of prisoners each year as reflected by the percentage of prisons in rural communities. So the communities, politicians, and for-profit prison providers collude to ensure that these communities remain vibrant on the backs of prisoners. The United States is an ideal market for a for-profit prison because it has surpassed the previous record-holder—the former Soviet Union—in the number of people it incarcerates. The more the United States incarcerates, the more private prisons profit. Considering the number and frequency of prisoners incarcerated in the United States, for-profit prison CEOs are not likely to let up on lobbying for stiffer laws. Furthermore, judging by the increasing prisoner population, their efforts seem to be paying off.

126

Campaign Financing and Lobbying

The idea that for-profit firms make campaign contributions to legislators' campaigns to influence criminal justice policy is problematic because private prisons exploit labor, trade on the stock exchange, and are used as an economic development tool. Scholars worry that a "prison lobby" will emerge with a focus on increasing its profits through lobbying and campaign contributions.[49] Their concerns are real when you examine the findings of a report by the National Institute on Money in State Politics:

> Privatized-corrections companies contributed more than $1,125,598 to **830** candidates in **fourteen** southern states in the 2000 election cycle. The total includes contributions from the companies, their executives and those in the lobbying firms representing the companies' electoral and legislative interests and was split **54** percent to **46** percent in favor of Democrats. These interests also split $96,432 almost evenly between political party committees in fourteen states, giving Republican committees 49 percent and Democratic committees 48 percent. The balance went to caucus committees. [emphasis in original source][50]

These findings are revealing because most of the campaign contributions have been given to legislators in southern states, exactly where most of the private prisons are located presently. I should add that there are private prisons in about thirty-one states according to the Bureau of Justice Statistics.[51] The point is, lobbying by for-profit prisons is working extremely well in southern states, and the practice is being replicated in other regions of the country. Privatization in southern states is aided by the fact that the South is not heavily unionized, so for-profit providers have been able to set-up shop without resistance. Additionally, because the southern region is extremely poor and without unions, the wages for-profit prisons pay correctional officers are not contested. Poor people are less inclined to turn down a job, even one with nominal benefits and pay.

Southern states also have some of the tougher laws on the book—laws that these for-profit providers have lobbied for since the opening

127

of their prisons in this region. Another interesting point is that the prison industry is not much different in its contributions than its fellow specific-interest industries:

the $1.1 million-plus contributed by private prisons interests to candidates in southern states is in line with the contributing levels of other specific-interest industries, such as gambling and casinos, which gave almost $1.1 million, or tobacco sales, which gave $737,496. But it is less than the amount given by liquor wholesalers, who gave $2.1 million; electric utilities, which gave $2.5 million; or insurance companies, which gave $5.3 million in the region.[52]

This data, gleaned from the *National Institute on Money in State Politics* report, reinforces my point that standard and state explanations are inadequate in explaining the prison privatization phenomenon. The campaign contributions data demonstrates the importance of examining broader issues, such as lobbying, and the role they play in decision-making.

Another reason that explains why standard explanations are insufficient—one that buttresses the argument of scholars concerned with development of a prison lobby—is supported by the following examples. The first example involves CCA, the second largest private provider of prisons, which was founded in 1983 by Nashville banker/financier Doctor R. Crants and Tennessee Republican Party chair Tom Beasley. Beasley used his political connections to secure early contracts, which would suggest that politics had more to do with who was better equipped to run the prison than who could do it cheaper or better. Through Beasley's lobbying, Governor Lamar Alexander of Tennessee attempted to help Beasley privatize the entire Tennessee prison system. Governor Alexander's wife, Honey Alexander, held stock in CCA as did Ned McWherter, the Speaker of the Tennessee House, who eventually became governor after Alexander.[53] Once their relationship was revealed, they disassociated themselves from the company because of the controversy surrounding their relationship with CCA.

Another example, provided by the National Institute on Money in State Politics, complements the previous data and shows the following major private-prison industry contributions breakdown during the 2000 election cycle:

- Corrections Corporation of America, which made more than 600 contributions totaling more than **$443,300** to candidates in **thirteen** of the fourteen states studied, excluding only South Carolina. CCA also gave **twenty-three** contributions totaling more than **$36,580** to state political party committees;

- Wackenhut Corrections (the largest corrections company in the industry), which gave 336 contributions totaling more than **$237,750** to candidates in **six** states—Arkansas, Florida, Louisiana, Mississippi, Oklahoma and Texas. Wackenhut made **eight** contributions to state political committees for **$33,850**;

- Cornell Corrections, which made **284** contributions totaling nearly **$100,000** in **three** states—Georgia, North Carolina and Texas. Cornell Corrections gave to state political party committees twice for a total of **$3,000**;

- Correctional Services Corp., which gave 208 contributions in **two** states—Florida and Texas—totaling more than **$97,670**. Correctional Services Corp. gave to state party committees **thirteen** times for a total of more than **$12,800**.[54]

Source: Edward Bender, "A Contributing Influence: The Private Prison Industry and Political Giving in South," The National Institute on Money in State Politics, 2002: 5.

Still another example of the tactics used by for-profit prisons to influence legislators is provided by former University of Florida professor Charles Thomas, who helped guide Florida into privatization.[55] Analysts assert that Professor Thomas' report on the private prison industry can influence the stock market because he has earned a reputation as the top expert in the field. However, they also point out that as Thomas' reputation has grown, so has his bankbook. Additionally, the Thomas' dealings embellish the point that private prisons are only in the business for money, and they will use every tool at their disposal to influence policy in favor of their industry. For instance, Thomas, an academic by profession and agent of for-profit prisons, was on the payroll of a private corrections company and commanded a $3 million consulting fee for a January 1999 merger involving CCA. This is problematic because he is considered the leading expert on prison privatization. Furthermore, "state records show that Professor Thomas owned an estimated $660,000 in stock in four private corrections companies and is a member of the board of directors for Prison Realty Corp., an REIT formed to provide financing for private corrections facilities."[56] When Thomas published a study with two other scholars stating that private prisons are more effective in reducing recidivism and released the report online, critics contended that it was done to influence the stock market and pursuade legislators who were considering privatization. The report is not considered to be credible because Thomas did not disclose that he is a consultant for the for-profit prisons; his relationship with the for-profit industry impeaches their findings.

The data provided by the National Institute on Money in State Politics shows that the idea that for-profit firms lobby for laws favorable to their industry is not unrealistic. More surprising is the fact that an academic has been co-opted to help them propagate the idea that for-profit prisons are the solution to the states overcrowding and financial problems. The plot thickens because now to go along with the communities, politicians, for-profit prison providers, we have academics financed by the for-profit prison sector to generate reports that influence the stock market and communities considering prison privatization.

These parties—the communities, politicians, for-profit prison providers, and academics—have come together to ensure that these for-profit prisons are successful; however, in many cases it may not be enough to guarantee the prisoners that keep profits and stock prices up. So, for-profit prisons are accused of using strategies that

130

make it difficult to earn "good time" credit, which, if awarded, would shorten a prisoner's stay. A shortened stay means less profits for private prison providers.

For-profit prison providers have seen success in their efforts to lobby legislators and shower them with campaign contributions in order to influence them to allow providers to build a prison, to give out private contracts to manage a prison, or to pass laws favorable to their industry. While no one has proven that campaign contributions influence policy makers, there is an extensive amount of circumstantial evidence to indicate that campaign contributions made by for-profit prisons providers do influence legislators to act in their best interest. For instance, Texas has the most private prisons in the United States, and the majority of them are in rural communities. Is it a coincidence that U.S. House Leader Tom DeLay, (R-Texas) "took a $100,000 check from a prison company at a Lexington fund-raiser in August 2004"?[57] Critics for prison privatization contend that this is no mere coincidence, but it is difficult to know whether or not the actions of DeLay and other politicians are connected to the contributions of private prison firms. What is known is that for-profit prisons back rural communities into a corner so they will see for-profit prisons as their savior; then, the prisons profit at the expense of the poor and minorities.

AMERICAN LEGISLATIVE EXCHANGE COUNCIL

Besides campaign contributions, for-profit providers have found another way to be more proactive in policy making. That conduit is ALEC, a Washington, DC-based public policy organization that supports conservative legislators[58] and allows for-profit providers to serve on the same Criminal Justice Task Force Committee as legislators. Founded in the 1970s, ALEC has facilitated the passage of hundreds of laws from tax cuts to loosened environmental regulations to longer prison sentences.[59]

Of the 2,400 state lawmakers, a little over two thirds are members of ALEC.[60] ALEC's primary focus is to develop model legislative proposals that advance conservative principals such as privatization. Membership in ALEC is very advantageous to for-profit providers of prisons. Why? They interact with conservatives who advocate

privatization and who also happen to be very law-and-order oriented. This is very propitious for for-profit providers because they are
sitting in the same criminal task force committee meetings as lawmakers who are responsible for policy making in the states they have
targeted for prison privatization.

Proof of ALEC's effectiveness in achieving its legislative agenda is
as follows: "In 1995–96, ALEC's model legislation resulted in 1,647
bills, including 365 that became law (a 22 percent success rate). By
1999, introduction of bills passed on ALEC's model had increased by
34 percent; of 2,208 bills, 322 were enacted into law."[61] It is safe to
assume that, because ALEC is a conservatively oriented organization
and the current administration is conservative and supports privatization, it is likely the ALEC success rate in crafting legislation that
becomes law may improve.

Crafting or drafting legislation requires time and money, so where
does ALEC get its funding from? Corporations, including for-profit
prison providers, put up the majority of the money to cover ALEC's
operating budget. As a result, just as foundations shape what is
researched when they award funds, corporations that donate money
also get to shape the political agenda of ALEC. As a form of quid pro
quo, they participate on the Criminal Justice Task Force Committee,
which considers many of the laws that affect their industry. For-profit
providers make campaign contributions, donate money to ALEC, and
serve on policy task forces that impact their industry. Rural communities with a vested interest in prisons are the beneficiaries of these
dealings.

Further proof of the legislative influence of for-profit providers can
be found in the amount of tough criminal justice legislation that
ALEC has supported. This kind of legislation has become ALEC's spe-
cialty, I suspect, because of the involvement and funding of for-profit
providers who benefit from such legislation.

The findings support critics who worry about a "prison lobby"
developing and bringing about a subgovernment change in the prison
industry. Their fears are realized when you examine the summary of
ALEC's criminal justice success.

As Table 5.2 demonstrates, ALEC has been very effective in
achieving its goals, including tougher criminal justice policy with a

Table 5.2
Impact of For-Profit Prisons' Lobbying

Legislation	Number of enactments	States
Truth in Sentencing Act (inmates serve at least 85% of their sentence)	25	Arkansas, California, Connecticut, Florida, Georgia, Illinois,Indiana, Louisiana, Massachusetts, Michigan, Mississippi, Missouri, Montana, Nevada, New Hampshire, North Carolina, North Dakota, Oklahoma, South Carolina, South Dakota, Tennessee, Texas, Virginia, West Virginia, Wyoming
Habitual Offender/ Three Strikes (life imprisonment for a third violent felony)	11	Arkansas, Florida, Indiana, Montana, New Jersey, North Carolina, South Carolina, Tennessee, Vermont, Virginia, Wyoming*
Private Correctional Facilities	4	Arkansas, Connecticut, Mississippi, Virginia
Prison Industries (requires prisoners to work for private companies)	1	Mississippi

* "Three Strikes" legislation was previously passed in Washington State in 1993 and California in 1994.

Source: Bridgette Sarabi, and Edward Bender, "The Prison Payoff: The Role of Politics and Private Prisons in the Incarceration Boom," Western Prison Project (November 2000): 4.

focus on the for-profit prison business. For-profit prisons have been very effective in permeating the culture of ALEC via funding and campaign contributions, and their efforts have been rewarded with passage of truth-in-sentencing and habitual offender/three-strikes legislation. ALEC's process of bringing a proposal to law has been summarized in seven steps by the American Radio Works documentary, *Corrections, Inc.* They capture the process by which for-profit prisons influence legislation through ALEC as a graphic model, represented in Figure 5.1.

With current societal problems like immigration and the use of the PATRIOT Act driving up the prison population, along with the punitive laws supported by state legislative members of ALEC, things look good for the for-profits prisons' future bottom-line. However, other implications of these laws are jobs for rural communities, votes for legislators in those rural communities, and campaign contributions to legislators. Everyone wins—except the prisoners in the for-profit prisons.

Keep in mind that for-profit providers of prisons are not the only contributors to ALEC who hope to influence prison privatization legislation. Many of the companies who have sprouted up in support of private prisons are contributing to ALEC to support their investment. ALEC and the American Correctional Association lists the following companies:[62]

- Ameritech
- AT&T
- Bayer (Sheffield Plastics Division)
- Bell Atlantic
- Bell South
- DuPont Company
- GlaxoSmithKline
- MCI
- Merck & Co.
- National Association of Bail Insurance Companies
- Schering Plough
- Sodexho Marriot (until recently a major investor in CCA; student protests on college campuses forced them to divest themselves of CCA)
- Sprint

Figure 5.1
Corporate Sponsored Crime Laws

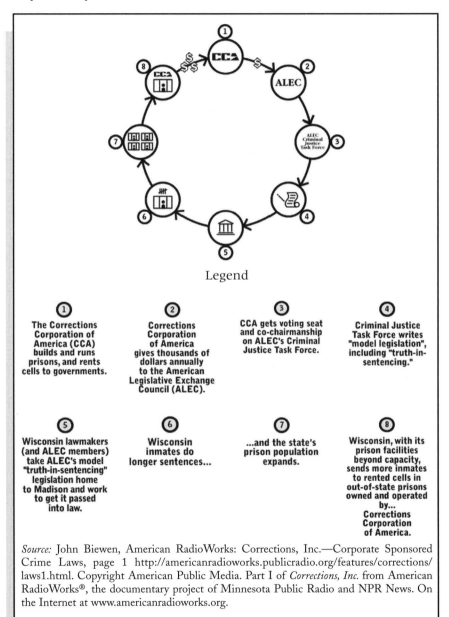

Legend

① **The Corrections Corporation of America (CCA) builds and runs prisons, and rents cells to governments.**

② **Corrections Corporation of America gives thousands of dollars annually to the American Legislative Exchange Council (ALEC).**

③ **CCA gets voting seat and co-chairmanship on ALEC's Criminal Justice Task Force.**

④ **Criminal Justice Task Force writes "model legislation", including "truth-in-sentencing."**

⑤ **Wisconsin lawmakers (and ALEC members) take ALEC's model "truth-in-sentencing" legislation home to Madison and work to get it passed into law.**

⑥ **Wisconsin inmates do longer sentences...**

⑦ **...and the state's prison population expands.**

⑧ **Wisconsin, with its prison facilities beyond capacity, sends more inmates to rented cells in out-of-state prisons owned and operated by... Corrections Corporation of America.**

Source: John Biewen, American RadioWorks: Corrections, Inc.—Corporate Sponsored Crime Laws, page 1 http://americanradioworks.publicradio.org/features/corrections/laws1.html. Copyright American Public Media. Part I of *Corrections, Inc.* from American RadioWorks®, the documentary project of Minnesota Public Radio and NPR News. On the Internet at www.americanradioworks.org.

- Turner Construction
- Quest (formerly US West)
- Pfizer

Basically, everyone is protecting their interest via ALEC, and the businesses feed off the profit behemoth prisons have become. With ALEC maintaining a focus on private prisons, corporate money should continue to find its way into its coffers, and laws that incapacitate prisoners for longer periods of time should continue to come out of the task forces that corporate members share with ALEC-affiliated legislators. It is obvious that corporate money is driving ALEC's policy agenda, and the prisoners continue to suffer in the name of profits.

Corrections-Commercial Complex

The corrections-commercial complex is described as the "criminal justice industrial complex." It has many of the same attributes as the "military-industrial complex," such as rising expenditures being spent on corrections, but it should be noted that spending on the criminal justice industrial complex in the past twenty years has grown twice as fast as military spending.[63] For instance, the three areas that comprise the criminal justice industrial complex—law enforcement, courts, and corrections—were estimated to have spent about $150 billion annually. According to the article "Cashing in on Crime," experts estimated that, if this trend was to continue, by 2002 annual expenditures would round out to about $200 billion annually for corrections.[64]

Spending is just one facet of the growing corrections-commercial complex. Employment opportunities are being created as a result of the ever-increasing emphasis on incarceration as opposed to rehabilitation. Additionally, corporations are cashing in on the correctional industry. Corporations advertise in trade newspapers devoted to the latest trends in corrections; they also participate in correctional trade shows, where prisons are sold the latest wares, such as prison fences that offer detection technology, toilets, blankets, and prisoner security transportation services.

Even telephone corporations like AT&T, Bell South, and MCI have discovered the prison industry market and are offering long-distance services. Prisoners are restricted to making collect calls, which translates into profits for the phone companies; "AT&T has an ad that reads: HOW HE GOT IN IS YOUR BUSINESS. HOW HE GETS OUT IS OURS. AT&T estimated that in 1995 prisoner's generated about $1 billion in long distance calls."[65] MCI installed free payphones throughout the California prison system and levied a $3 surcharge on each phone call made; the prisoner's family picked up the tab, and the California Department of Corrections received 32 percent of the profits from MCI.[66] It has been reported that communication companies charge prisoners six times the normal charges when they use prison payphones. Furthermore, companies such as AT&T, Sprint, and MCI can generate profits in the range of $15,000 per payphone per day in a prison.[67] It should be clear why corporations lobby ALEC—prisons are a billion-dollar industry with unlimited profit-making opportunities in the current climate.

Corporations also exploit prisoners by charging "basic necessities such as medical care, toilet paper, and the use of the law library."[68] This could be seen as reasonable if the prisoners made a livable wage. However, even though prisoners help corporations earn millions of dollars through their labor, they are paid wages comparable to the slave system, convict lease system, and sharecropping arrangement. So, the 50 cents they receive after all deductions have been taken out of their checks must be used to pay for toilet paper, the library, and medical services.

Still another area of exploitation is the number of public works projects prisoners are involved in during their incarceration. An irony of prison privatization is that prisoners have become valuable in the eyes of rural communities, for-profit prisons, and corporations. Things have really changed for prisoners, who used to be viewed as worthless. Now they help companies make millions of dollars—in some cases, billions of dollars.

Finally, to get an idea of the business machine prisons have become, all one has to do is examine the number of companies involved in selling good and services to jails and prisons. To get an idea of the number of businesses involved in the prison industry, look at the Standard & Poor's Register of Corporations, Directors, and Executives and its Corporate Description—known as the S&P Registers—and the American Correctional Association (ACA) Buyers' Guide.[69] The organizations list biographical and business-related information about corporations, and you will find that many of them are involved in the prison industry.

Benefits for Rural Communities

Along with the ever-growing prison population, there has been a rural prison boom, which translates into "a substantial transfer of economic and political power from urban to rural America."[70] The reason for this is an obscure provision in the census that states that prisoners are enumerated in the populations of the towns and counties in which they are incarcerated and not in the communities from which they came. The impact of this provision is that urban communities, from which the majority of prisoners are taken, will lose out on nearly $2 trillion in federal funds tied to population counts. Instead, these funds will go to the rural towns where many of the for-profit prisons are situated.

The economic development benefits of a prison for rural communities are brought into focus by the Prison Policy Initiative[71]:

- While urban counties that export prisoners lose census population, rural counties importing them gain census population.

- While rural legislators serve only their nonincarcerated population, urban legislators must serve their nonincarcerated population plus those they exported for incarceration.

- While urban areas lose legislators, their rural counterparts gain them.

According to the data in the Prison Policy Initiative,[72] state policies tend to be "skewed toward the interests of rural residents in prison hosting areas and against the interests of urban residents." Another benefit for rural communities housing prisoners is the federal dollars transferred from urban centers to rural centers for "Medicaid, foster care, adoption assistance and social services block grants and 169 other programs."[73] Additionally, prisoners' low income make these rural communities look poorer than they are, which makes them eligible for additional federal poverty-related grants. Prisoners that are counted in these rural communities also impact the way legislative districts are drawn; prisoners are usually reapportioned to mostly rural and Republican areas—and Republicans are on record stating that they support privatization. In essence, prisoners end up in communities where they have no representation, and legislators interact with ALEC to keep these prisoners incarcerated for longer periods of time by lobbying for stiffer sentences and to kill parole and probation. Everyone benefits except the prisoners, their families, and the communities they left. For rural communities, the census plus prisoners equals dollars and representation.

FELONY DISENFRANCHISEMENT

As political power is transferred to rural communities when they import urban prisoners, economic power is transferred as well. Legislators use the newfound prisoner population to redraw lines and gain seats. The interesting aspect of this is that the urban prisoners who are transferred to these rural communities cannot vote; their inability to vote while incarcerated means they cannot vote against many of the laws that legislators institute to keep them incarcerated for longer periods of time. Many of them have lost the right to vote permanently, depending on the state to which they return. They are treated on paper as residents and citizens, but they are not accorded the rights of residents during their stay in prison.

Many prisoners return to their communities of origin stripped of resources—the dollars that followed them to prison do not return when they come home because so many of them end up homeless and difficult for the census to count. Others return to prison because they lack the support system, skills, and community resources to help reintegrate them back into the community. They will never benefit from social services because those dollars were also transferred to the rural communities where they served their time. The resources are inadequate to help facilitate their reintegration because these dollars remain in the rural communities once the prisoners return home, until the next census is taken. In the meantime, they are faced with bleak prospects. A felony record, especially a drug conviction, negatively impacts their ability to matriculate to college. What is fascinating here is that the United States, the most democratic and free country, is the only democracy in the world that deprives its citizens of suffrage after they have completed their sentence. According to the NACLA Report on the Americas, "coupled with the unprecedented rate of incarceration, disenfranchisement laws fundamentally restructure political power and entrench the politicians who support and benefit from drug war policies."[74] For instance, in the 2000 presidential elections in Florida, "200,000 African-American men (31 percent of all African-American men in the state) were barred from that election, as they will be from every other election forever."[75] If they had gained the right to vote in Governor Jeb Bush's state, data suggests the outcome of the election may have been different for his brother, President George W. Bush, because most of the African American felons would more than likely have voted Democratic. This is an important element in this discussion because Florida is one of the main actors in the prison privatization movement. By reobtaining the right to vote, these former prisoners could sit a legislature less inclined toward conservative justice policy. This is not to say that I want prisoners making laws that do not punish them, but I would like to see laws that are just and equitable and cease punishing when time has been served. I am against the commodification of crime and the commodification of human beings, which strips them permanently of their humanity. I am especially concerned about nonviolent offenders, not violent offenders.

The court agrees that there is a disproportionate incarceration of African American males. For instance, "in *Farrakhan v. Washington*, the court found that a 'statistical disproportionality' in the racial composition of prison populations constitutes a form of discrimination of the 1982 Voting Rights Act."[76] So the "war on drugs" and "get tough crime" campaigns, which have disproportionately impacted African Americans, also can be viewed as discriminatory considering that "whites and blacks use drugs at almost exactly the same rate."[77] According to the article "Collateral Damage in the War on Drugs,"

140

"because there are five times as many whites as blacks in the United States, it follows that the overwhelming majority of drug users are white."[78] As a result of targeting by police departments, African Americans are admitted to prison at a rate 13.4 times greater than whites.[79] Rural communities benefit from this unjust targeting; for-profit prisons and rural communities that use prisons for economic development are not concerned about the practices that ensnare African Americans disproportionately and take away resources from their communities. Their only concerns are jobs and profits, regardless of the impact on others. Jobs and profits are foremost in the minds of rural communities, not the impact these practices have on others, especially African Americans.

Laws were fashioned to incarcerate blacks in the 1800s up until the 1960s for the purpose of extracting free labor and circumventing laws that enfranchised blacks, and it appears that these Jim Crow practices have returned in the form of the "war on drugs" and the "get tough on crime" campaigns, stripping away the hard-won concessions blacks received from the U.S. government. Once blacks were freed, there was no way to exploit the labor that they provided as slaves; hence, ordinances in the 1800s were devised to recapture that labor. Because blacks had no jobs, laws were passed that punished vagrancy and loitering. By passing these laws, southern whites were able to recapture much of the labor they lost during slavery. History is repeating itself; the law is once again being used as an instrument to enslave blacks to recapture labor.

Prison labor is reminiscent of the sharecropping system because prisoners work and make million of dollars for corporations, but at the end of the day they have nothing to show for their labor. Prisoners should make restitution to the victims, pay for their incarceration, be able to save money to tide them over after their release, and be able to send money home to their families. Prisoners should have the right to negotiate the wages they are paid based on their skill level. The practice of exploiting labor has to stop.

During the Jim Crow era, blacks were deprived of the right to vote, and about 13 percent of black males have lost the right to vote presently. By losing the right to vote, prisoners are further humiliated upon their return to their communities. They have lost years of their lives in prison, plus they have lost the right to vote, the right to an education, and the right to employment. The negative impact prisons have on inmates are the same as they were during the Jim Crow era, and that is why the drug war and the "tough on crime" campaigns are considered Jim Crow's grandsons. These prisoners, affected by the current practices of for-profit prisons and ALEC, are likely to return to prison because the system of justice in the United States does not afford second chances to minorities. White inmates are more likely to rebound from their incarceration, but minorities are targeted by these profiteers of human misery. According to the employment study "The Mark of a Criminal Record," "among blacks without criminal records, only 14% received callbacks, relative to 34% of white noncriminals."[80] Even more troubling is the fact that "even whites *with* criminal records received more favorable treatment (17%) than blacks *without* criminal records (14%)."[81] For-profit providers of prisons would not have it any other way. That is why they lobby for stiffer sentences, reduction in probation and parole, and the suspension of Pell Grants to ex-prisoners, specifically those with drug convictions. In effect, the impediments that have put in place via ALEC set the prisoners up for a return to prison.

The Higher Education Act

Under the Higher Education Act (HEA) of 1998, "federal financial aid, including loans, grants and work study, is denied to any student convicted of a drug related offense."[82] According to the article "Collateral Damage in the War on Drugs," "given that 55 percent of those convicted of drug offenses are black, and the fact that this law will not affect the wealthy who do not need financial aid, the HEA plainly targets low income people of color."[83] An even more telling indictment of this act is that murder and rape does not render a person ineligible for financial aid, but getting convicted while possessing small amounts of marijuana does.[84] *The Student Guide to Financial Aid*, which is published by the Department of Education, states that "the law suspends aid eligibility for students convicted under federal or state law of selling or possessing illegal drugs."[85] Denying financial aid to convicted drug offenders is a shrewd way to ensure future minority prisoners.

In a technologically advanced economy, the outlook is extremely bleak for former inmates without a college degree. Depriving offenders, especially nonviolent offenders, of another opportunity to better themselves is an excellent way to guarantee they return to prison. Again, because of lobbying accomplished through ALEC, which is an arm of the for-profit prisons, young men and women of color are being set up to return to prison under the guise of the war on drugs—a campaign to extract cheap labor and prop up rural white communities devastated by deindustrialization. At some point, the for-profit prisons and legislators have to be taken to task for depriving citizens who have gone astray of the opportunity of a second chance. We would not have the privilege of President George W. Bush's leadership if he were not given a second chance. He made mistakes in his "youthful exuberance," so why can't poor kids get a similar second chance? Bush's niece, Governor Jeb Bush's daughter, was caught with the same amount of crack cocaine that, for most minorities, results in a five-year jail sentence under the federal sentencing guidelines, even though it is a first offense for many of them.

Summary

Key individuals or groups of individuals in society press for and facilitate prison privatization—the policy community or "policy entrepreneurs." This community is instrumental in shaping the policy agenda and policy formulation. There are plenty of studies examining the workings of the policy formulation process and providing observations on the policy-making process. These include studies of subsystems, networks, and iron triangles, which have all been associated with determining who actually affects what ideas are moved to the forefront to potentially become policies. In the for-profit prison arena, legislators, CEOs of for-profit prisons firms, and members of ALEC all determine what gets on the corrections policy agenda through ALEC's Criminal Justice Task Force Committee. The "policy entrepreneurs"—in this case the for-profit prison CEOs and their lobbyists—market the ideas and proposals that actually get attention within the ALEC Criminal Justice Task Force Committee. Tireless pressing of their ideals, continuous campaign contributions, timing, and readiness all help them sell the idea that for-profit prisons are the way to solve prison overcrowding. Traumatization from 9/11 has made the public extremely phobic concerning safety. As a result of the understandable fear that has paralyzed the country, laws are not being challenged as much as they should be. This means that ALEC and the current administration have been able to pass lots of laws that will guarantee that for-profit prisons remain a fixture in our future.

Supporting imprisonment as a means to extract free labor, even in the face of the Thirteenth Amendment, these groups have targeted the poor to enslave, depriving them of an education, commodifying their bodies, disenfranchising them, and turning them into economic development fodder. Legislators, rural communities, interest groups, lobbyists, and Wall Street are all complicit in fueling the imprisonment boom. Community livelihood, 401 (k) plans, and corporations have become tied to an industry that exploits the poor, their families, and their communities.

Chapter Six

State of Prison Privatization and Conclusions

Are States Still Pursuing Prison Privatization?

For-profit prisons have been growing in the United States, and they have moved beyond the Atlantic and Pacific to countries like Australia, South Africa, Israel, and Great Britain; Germany is beginning the process of contracting its prisons. Because private prisons have a built-in incentive to lock up more prisoners, keep them longer, and reduce rehabilitation programs to maximize profits, this should guarantee that they have a future in our country. This is not to say that that for-profit prisons are not adversely affected by the business cycle; in the late 1990s, their business was shaken by excessive escapes and well-publicized abuse cases.

On the other hand, coupled with increasing federal privatization and the crackdown on terrorism and immigration, the outlook seems promising for private prisons. It is likely that criminal justice policy increasingly will be driven by the profit motive as private prisons continue to attempt to strengthen their stock prices with the current attitude of punishment first. Additionally, as long as ALEC remains an arm of the for-profit prison firms and legislators continue to serve on the same committee as the for-profit firms who continue to provide campaign contributions, I predict that states will continue to endorse prison privatization.

Data provided by the Bureau of Justice Statistics from 2000 through 2003 support the idea that for-profit prisons have been growing in the United States and that states are still pursuing prison privatization. For instance, at midyear 2000 there were 76,010 inmates held in private facilities, in 2001 there were 94,948, and in 2002 there were 86,626, a slightly lower number of inmates than the previous year. However, in 2003 the number of inmates held in private facilities went back up to 94,361.[1] My belief is shared by an Associated Press writer who points out that although "state governments are no longer fueling a private prison boom, the industry's major companies are upbeat—thanks in large measure to a surge of business from federal agencies seeking to house fast-rising numbers of criminals and detained aliens."[2] States will continue to pursue privatization but not at the same dizzying pace as before.

Since the 1990s, prison overcrowding has not changed; thus, states will continue to pursue prison privatization because of budget problems many have not been able to resolve. Until the laws are changed, overcrowding will continue to be a problem for states, and the for-profit prisons will hover like vultures. Furthermore, "the industry's future is bright enough that the Geo Group (formerly Wackenhut) is buying rival Correctional Services Corp., but prospects hinge largely on incarceration trends."[3] However, as long as states continue to balk at funding new prisons despite the fact that incarceration rates continue to increase, the war on drugs continues unabated, and the government continues to use the PATRIOT Act to detain suspected terrorist and immigrants, for-profit firms should continue to be a part of the states' future.

What Problems Exist for Prison Privatization?

Although the outlook seems positive for the prison privatization industry growing and prospering, there are several potential problems that could undermine the industry. Lack of basic health care, human rights violations, persistent fiscal problems for states, and safety issues (including abuse, assaults, escapes, and the inability to attract and retain qualified correctional guards) are landmines for

for-profit prisons. If left unattended, these problems may eventually lead to the demise of for-profit prisons again.

HEALTH CARE

Although prison officials are obligated under the Eighth Amendment to provide prisoners with adequate medical and mental health care[4] while incarcerated, in many cases this is not happening. Additionally, for-profit health care has become a popular choice for prisons across the states. The same sort of arguments, such as cost-effectiveness, are driving states and localities to privatize health care, "but an examination of the record shows that this method has been a disaster, not only for the incarcerated whose care has been precarious at best and too often injurious at worst, but also to the responsible governments that have been repeatedly sued, losing millions in damages awards and settlements."[5] For instance, "a yearlong examination of Prison Health [a for-profit health care provider] by *The New York Times* reveals repeated instances of medical care that has been flawed and sometimes lethal. The company has paid millions of dollars in fines and settlements."[6]

Moreover, New York State has really been impacted by Prison Health's incompetence because in "two deaths, and eight others across upstate New York, state investigators say they kept discovering the same failings: medical staffs trimmed to the bone, doctors underqualified or out of reach, nurses doing tasks beyond their training, prescription drugs withheld, patient records unread and employee misconduct unpunished."[7] Prison Health has an extremely poor record of providing health care in prisons, but it should be stated that the practices of Prison Health are a microcosm of the state of healthcare in for-profit prisons. The deaths in Prison Health facilities are not difficult to explain when you think about the level of inhumanity the nurses and doctors exhibit toward the patients. For example, the *New York Times* report cites the following acts of inhumanity:

an unlicensed doctor (not licensed in New York State) from Washington state in 2001 oversaw healthcare in several upstate New York jails and he continually overruled the doctors there, and he refused drugs and treatments to patients in the prisons;

a forty-six-year-old Rochester woman jailed in 2000 on a parole violation, died when her withdrawal from heroin went untreated for two days as she lay in her own vomit and excrement in the Monroe County Jail, moaning and crying for help and the nurses did not call a doctor or even clean her off; a premature baby was fished out of the toilet in the maternity unit of Albany County Jail by the guards, as the guards worked to revive the baby, the nurse stood by, offering little help.[8]

California has also had its share of problems with health care providers in prison. For instance, an eighty-pound inmate died at their Corcoran facility because he had not eaten for forty days.[9] The state was warned concerning the problems in this facility by a watchdog organization that evaluated the prison the year before the inmate's death, but officials failed to act and address the report's findings. The unfortunate part is that this kind of behavior is not the exception but the rule in many for-profit firms, which look for ways to cut costs at the expense of an inmate's well-being. If these firms continue to have publicized problems, for-profit prisons may, at some point, become a bad investment because the public may gain a conscience and initiate a divestiture campaign similar to the ones launched against South Africa's apartheid regime in the 1980s, against Yale University and several other universities in the United States, and Sodexho Marriott in this decade.

HUMAN RIGHTS

For-profit prisons have done a poor job of protecting an inmate's civil and human rights. There are documented cases of physical mistreatment, excessive disciplinary sanctions, inhumane physical conditions, and insufficient medical and mental health care in many jails, prisons, immigration detention centers, and juvenile detention facilities across the United States. Many of these same facilities are unclean and unsafe because of the cost-cutting practices of the for-profit prisons. Inmates are not accorded access to exercise and fresh air; in some instances, they are locked up in their windowless cells for twenty-three hours.

Moreover, an even worse dilemma for for-profit prisons is the number of deaths, rapes, and torture incidents captured in print and on reel that expose these problems. This has brought more scrutiny from the states and public, and, in some cases, the poor human rights record of for-profit prisons has resulted in lost contracts. A good example of a state canceling a contract because of human rights abuses is the case in the Esmor Corporation contract for the Elizabeth, New Jersey, immigration detention center.

In some cases, medical care in for-profit prisons is withheld because the guards speculate that the inmates are attempting to get out of work (although for-profit prisons claim work is voluntary). As a result, inmates have died on numerous occasions. If the inmate body count continues to grow in for-profit prisons, states will have to address these issues because there is the potential for litigation. The state cannot contract out its liability: they are ultimately responsible for the inmate's well-being whether he or she is in a public or private prison. Too many cases of human rights abuse reflect poorly on the for-profit firm and the contracting local, state, and federal agencies. This kind of negative publicity would not be good for a private prison's business or their stock. They have managed to survive so far; however, the situation is threatening for-profit firms' ability to grow because states and local agencies are hesitant to work with these for-profit prisons because of their poor record on human rights.

STATE FINANCES

As states continue to have fiscal problems, many have considered repealing laws like mandatory sentencing because they can no longer afford to keep these laws on the books. This does not bode well for private prisons. In addition, as a result of their fiscal problems, legislators are thinking in terms of being *smart* on crime instead of *tough* on crime. For instance, "in the past year, about 25 states have passed laws eliminating some of the lengthy mandatory minimum sentences so popular in the 1980s and 1990s, restoring early release for parole and offering treatment instead of incarceration for some drug offenders."[10] This is another potential inimical practice that would have serious consequences for the for-profit firms if states continue to repeal the stringent laws that have emaciated their budgets.

The repealing of laws such as mandatory sentencing, three strikes, and other punitive laws could possibly be very harmful to for-profit prisons' ability to grow outside the southern region of the country. If this trend continues, it is difficult to determine what the future holds for for-profit prisons. However, most of the states that are repealing these laws (Washington, Michigan, Iowa, Missouri, and Wisconsin) are outside the South; many of the South's problems—especially their fiscal problems—are more pronounced than the states that are repealing mandatory sentencing laws. The South remains firm in continuing the practice of using prisons as an economic development tool. The South was the last to free the slaves, and I do not see them releasing their twenty-first century slaves—prisoners—anytime soon.

SAFETY

Safety has become a serious issue for the for-profit prisons because of their unwillingness to pay to attract quality employees. For-profit prisons pay less than public prisons at the entry level as well as at the maximum pay level. Their turnover rate is three times higher than public prisons, and public prison corrections officers complete more preservice training hours than for-profit prison correctional officers (see Table 6.1).[11]

Critics have linked for-profit firms' inability to attract quality, educated employees to many of the abuses that take place in their facilities, including the use of restrictive devices on prisoners past justifiable safety considerations, sexual assaults, and other incidents

Table 6.1
Correctional Officer Chart

	Public	Private
Correctional officer entry level salary (average)	$23,002	$17,628
Correctional officer max level salary (average)	$36,328	$22,082
Correctional officer turnover rate (average)	16%	52.2%
Preservice correctional officer training (hours)	250	153

Source: Corrections Yearbook, 2000.

of rampant abuse. Critics also point to the fact that many of the for-profit prisons are understaffed and, because they are severely over-crowded, the ratio of correctional officers to prisoners is unacceptable. Because the prisons are undermanned, correctional officers are unable to cut down on sexual abuse, fights, and inmate escapes and cannot handle medical emergencies. If for-profit prisons are plagued by publicly documented safety problems, will states continue to export prisoners to these facilities? It is highly unlikely; therefore, safety is a key concern for-profit prisons if they hope to stay in this industry and continue to prosper.

There are a number of issues that may turn the public against for-profit prisons, but these are the more salient ones. So far, these prisons have managed to stay in business and, in some regions, expand their operations despite these problems. Only time will provide an answer regarding whether private prisons will be abolished again as they were in the 1800s.

Recurring Debates about Prison Privatization

The issue of whether privatization is a viable alternative continues to be debated across the United States. The arguments have not changed, and the ability to save taxpayers money is at the forefront of this debate. As recently as February 2005, an effort was made to privatize the entire prison system in my hometown of Memphis, Tennessee. In the 1980s, CCA was unsuccessful in their bid to privatize the entire prison system in Nashville, which is also their head-quarters. CCA has moved west to Memphis in hopes of finding less resistance. Much to their chagrin, the resistance to privatization has been just as strong in Memphis.

Another point of debate is whether for-profit prisons should publicly trade their stock. Many attack this question from a moral perspective: Because for-profit prisons trade on the stock exchange, do they have a vested interest to incarcerate? The answer to this question is clearly yes. Debate continues to take place regarding whether the state should give up its punishment responsibility to an entity that benefits financially from punishment. For instance, for-profit prison providers punish inmates with loss of "good time credit" for not working in prison, despite the fact that work is supposed to be voluntary. Fortunately, states are putting in place measures to monitor the for-profit prisons practices to ensure they are not engaging in activities designed to maximize their profits at the expense of prisoners and that they are meting out punishments fairly. Recently, however, monitors have been co-opted by the for-profit prison firms. This recurring issue is being addressed because when monitors are co-opted, the states' accountability monitoring is compromised. Monitors are an important check in the system; they ensure that the for-profit prisons adhere to the contract and guidelines the government has stipulated. Because the government does not contract out is liability, monitors help the government protect itself from lawsuits as well as loss of control of its agents. This is critical if abuse, safety, and human rights are going to improve in for-profit prison.

A final issue that has not been settled and continues to plague policy makers is the concern that the profit motive interferes with the democratic process in ways that are detrimental to society and prisoners. The existing process, in which for-profit firms achieve their goals through ALEC, impacts the political process negatively because it circumvents and skews the political process of checks and balances. Citizens should still be included in the decision regarding whether or not a prison should be built in their community, but citizens are being removed from the democratic process because legislatures no longer seek bonds to build prisons; they go directly to Wall Street for financing. Prisons impact quality of life and other issues that citizens hold dear. The system breaks down when a layer of checks and balances is removed as it has been in the for-profit prison environment. I should add that this is not applicable to all citizens; clearly citizens in rural communities are not concerned with how prisons are financed and built. Rural residents will appreciate this when they decide that they no longer want a prison in their community. How do they get rid of a privately built prison? With the check being removed because of private financing, it may be extremely difficult. Furthermore, the current process feeds the distrust that citizens have of their government, a distrust which has been growing over the last thirty years.

Figure 6.1
Circular Relationship of Convict Labor to Trend to Privatization with Profit Motive

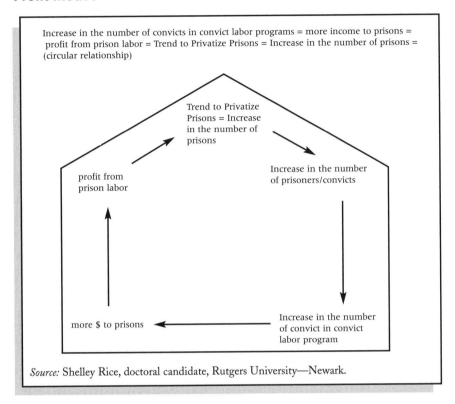

Increase in the number of convicts in convict labor programs = more income to prisons = profit from prison labor = Trend to Privatize Prisons = Increase in the number of prisons = (circular relationship)

Trend to Privatize Prisons = Increase in the number of prisons

profit from prison labor

Increase in the number of prisoners/convicts

more $ to prisons

Increase in the number of convict in convict labor program

Source: Shelley Rice, doctoral candidate, Rutgers University—Newark.

Concluding Remarks

I have attempted to demonstrate the circular relationship of convict labor and the trend to privatize with the profit motive serving as the impetus. The data supports the circular nature of this relationship. An increase in the number of convicts in convict labor programs leads to more income to prisons, which equals more profit from prison labor, which results in a trend to privatize prisons, which drives an increase in the number of prisons, which leads back to the beginning of the cycle: more convicts.[12]

Convict labor generates billions of dollars for UNICOR (the trade name of Federal Prison Industries, Inc.) and the California prison industry, two of the larger prison industries in the United States. A literature search reveals that more than forty states operate a prison industry program, and each of these industries is profitable. As the thirst for prison labor has increased, so has the effort to privatize prisons. States continue to suffer from overcrowding, and federal privatization is increasing along with the inmate population. As privatization and the prison population increase, so does the number of prisoners available for labor. The quest for profit drives this circular relationship.

I have attempted to illustrate that convict labor replaces the workforce laid off due to globalization, which has eroded the wages American workers can demand. Increases in union demands and strikes has driven businesses to replace disgruntled employees with inmate labor. Businesses now depend on cheap inmate labor to help them remain competitive and fill in the gaps during a downward turn of the business cycle. As a result, a circular relationship exists in the business cycle as legislators seek laws through ALEC to increase the inmate population and seek privatization of prisons. When the business cycle is trending downward, there is an increase in unemployment, an upswing in crime, and legislation to increase prisons;[13] for-profit prisons and communities attempt to take advantage of inmate labor when the business cycle is trending upward or downward.

Finally, I have attempted to show that the efficiency, effectiveness, and quality arguments pale in importance when the real reasons for states' prison privatization decisions are on the table. I have attempted to link legislators, communities, and interest groups to the drive to privatize. Profits drive their campaign, and it is at the expense of the prisoners.

Notes

Introduction

1. Adrian Moore, *Private Prisons: Quality Corrections at a Lower Cost,* Policy Study No. 240, Reason Public Policy Institute. http://www.reason.org/ps240.pdf, 1–43; Stephen Moore and Stuart M. Butler, *Privatization: A Strategy for Taming the Federal Budget* (Washington, DC: Heritage Foundation, 1987), 1; Ronald C. Moe, "Exploring the Limits of Privatization," *Public Administration Review* 47, no. 6 (1987): 453–60.
2. See Douglas McDonald, Carl Patten, Elizabeth Fournier, and Stephen Crawford, *Government's Management of Private Prisons* (Cambridge, MA: Abt Associates Inc., September 15, 2003), 1–102.
3. Ibid., 35.
4. See David Shichor, *Punishment for Profit: Private Prisons/Public Concerns* (Thousand Oaks, CA: Sage, 1995), 1–321; David Shichor, "The Corporate Context of Private Prisons," *Crime, Law and Social Change* 20, no. 2 (1993): 113–38.
5. See Travis C. Pratt and Jeff Maahs, "Are Private Prisons More Cost Effective Than Public Prisons? A Meta-Analysis of Evaluation Research Studies," *Crime and Delinquency,* September 1, 1999: 358–71
6. Philip Mattera and Mafruza Khan with Greg LeRoy and Kate Davis, *Jail Breaks: Economic Development Subsidies Given to Private Prisons* (Washington, DC: Good Jobs First/Institute on Taxation and Economic Policy, October 2001), 28, http://www.goodjobsfirst.org/jbstudy.htm.

Chapter One

1. See Ali Farazmand, ed., *Privatization or Public Enterprise Reform? International Case Studies with Implications for Public Management* (Westport, CT: Greenwood, 2001), 35; Samuel J. Brakel, "Prison Management, Private Enterprise Style: The Inmates Evaluation," *The England Journal of Criminal and Civil Confinement* 14, no. 2 (1988): 175–244.

2. See Ali Farazmand, "State Tradition and Public Administration in Iran in Ancient and Contemporary Perspectives," Handbook of Comparative and Development Public Administration, ed. A. Farazmand (New York: Marcel Dekker, 1991), 261; A. T. Olmstead, *History of the Persian Empire: The Achaemenid Period* (Chicago: University of Chicago Press, 1948), 25.

3. Ibid., 42.

4. R. Becker, "The Privatization of Prisons," *Prisons Today and Tomorrow*, ed. J. M. Pollack (Gaithersburg, MD: Aspen, 1997), 402.

5. Ibid.

6. Phil Smith, "Private Prisons: Profits of Crime," *Covert Action Quarterly*, Fall 1993, http://shadow.mediafilter.org/MFF/Prison.html.

7. See G. Rusche and O. Kircheimer, *Punishment and Social Structure* (New York: Columbia University Press, 1939), 80–81.

8. See David Fogel and Joe Hudson, *Justice as Fairness: Perspectives on the Justice Model* (Cincinnati: Anderson, 1981).

9. National Institute of Law Enforcement and Criminal Justice 1978, http://www.ojp.usdoj.gov.

10. See Farazmand, *Privatization or Public Enterprise Reform*, 53.

11. Ibid.

12. Note the pamphlet by David S. Greenberg, *The Problem of Prisons* (Philadelphia: American Friends Service Committee, 1971).

13. See John Irwin and James Austin, *It's About Time: America's Imprisonment Binge* (Belmont, CA: Wadsworth, 1994), 7.

14. See Patrick A. Langan, "America's Soaring Prison Population," *Science* 251 (March 29, 1991): 1568–73; Shichor, *Punishment for Profit*, 101.

15. See Research Roundup, *Private and Public Prisons: U.S. General Accounting Office* (Research Roundup: Spectrum, Summer 1997), 2.

16. See Pratt and Maahs, "Are Private Prisons More Cost-Effective," 358–71.

17. See David F. Linowes, *Privatization: Toward More Effective Government*, (Urbana and Chicago: University of Illinois Press, 1988), quoted in David Sichor, *Punishment for Profit: Private Prisons, Public Concerns* (London: SAGE Publications, 1995), 1.

18. See Brian B. Evans. "Private Prisons," *Emory Law Journal* 36 (1987): 253–283.

19. See U.S. Government Accounting Office (GAO), *Private Prisons* (Washington, DC: U.S. Government Printing Office, 1991), 19.

20. See Thomas Hobbes' 1651 book *Leviathan*; John Locke's 1690 *Two Treatises on Government*; and Jean-Jacques Rousseau's 1762 *Du Contract Social*.

Notes

21. See Geoffrey F. Segal and Adrian T. Moore, *Weighing the Watchman: Evaluating the Costs and Benefits of Outsourcing Correctional Services: Part II: Reviewing the Literature on Cost and Quality Comparisons*, Policy Study No. 290, Reason Public Policy Institute, 17.

22. See Shichor, "The Corporate Context," 113–38.

23. See American Federation of State, County, and Municipal Employee (AFSCME), "The Evidence Is Clear: Crime Shouldn't Pay," http://www.afscme.org/private/evidtc.htm.

24. See D. Shichor and M. J. Gilbert, "How Much Is Too Much Privatization in Criminal Justice?" *Privatization in Criminal Justice: Past, Present, and Future* (Cincinnati: Anderson, 2001), 85.

25. See S. R. Donizer, ed., *The Real War on Crime: The Report of the National Criminal Justice Commission* (New York: Harper Perennial Library, 1996), 22; S. Walker, *Popular Justice: A History of American Criminal Justice* (New York: Oxford University Press, 1980), 32.

26. Eric Bates, "Prisons for Profit," *The Nation* 26, no. 1 (1998): 8–11.

27. See Douglas McDonald, Elizabeth Fournier, Malcolm Russell-Einhorn, and Stephen Crawford, *Private Prisons in the United States: An Assessment of Current Practice* (Cambridge, MA: Abt Associates Inc., July 16, 1998), 53.

28. See American Federation of State, County, and Municipal Employee (AFSCME), "The Evidence Is Clear: Crime Shouldn't Pay," http://www.afscme.org/private/evidtc.htm.

29. See Irwin and Austin, *It's About Time*, 1–256.

30. See William C. Butcher, "The Privatization of Prisons in Representative Democracies: Let the People Decide" (thesis, Troy State University, Fort Bragg, 1997), 8.

31. See John McLaughlin, "Going Private," *National Review*, February 1996: 24.

32. Charles T. Goodsell, "The Grace Commission: Seeking Efficiency for the Whole People?" *Public Administration Review* 44 (May/June 1984): 196–203.

33. Pratt and Maahs, "Are Private Prisons More Cost-Effective," 358–372.

34. Sean McConville, "Aid From Industry? Private Corrections and Prison Crowding," *America's Correctional Crisis: Prison Populations and Public Policy*, eds. Stephen D. Gottfredson and Sean McConville (New York: Greenwood, 1987).

35. Pratt and Maahs, "Are Private Prisons More Cost-Effective," 358–372.

36. David B. Bobrow and John S. Dryzek, *Policy Analysis by Design* (Pittsburgh: University of Pittsburgh Press, 1987), 205.

37. R. Becker, "The Privatization of Prisons," *Prisons Today and Tomorrow*, ed. J. M. Pollack (Gaithersburg, MD: Aspen, 1997), 402.

38. See Charles H. Logan and Sharla. P. Rausch, "Punish and Profit: The Emergence of Private Enterprise Prisons," *Justice Quarterly* 2 (1985): 303–318; T. D. Hutto, "The Privatization of Prisons," *Are Prisons Any Better? Twenty Years of Correctional Reform*, ed. John W. Murphy and Jack E. Dison (Newbury Park, CA: Sage, 1990), 77–93.

39. Alex M. Durham, "The Future of Correctional Privatization: Lessons From the Past," *Privatizing Correctional Institutions*, eds. Gary W. Bowman, Simon Hakim, and Paul Seidenstat (New Brunswick, NJ: Transaction, 1993), 33–49.

40. Cited in Steven Wisotsky, "A Society of Suspects: The War on Drugs and Civil Liberties," *Cato Policy Analysis No. 180*, https://www.cato.org/pubs/pas/pa-180.html. The author cited by the Cato report is Ted Gest, "The Prison Boom Bust," *U.S. News and World Report*, May 4, 1992: 28.

41. Norman R. Cox and William E. Osterhoff, "The Public-Private Partnership: A Challenge and an Opportunity for Corrections," *Privatizing Correctional Institutions*, eds. Gary W. Bowman, Simon Hakim, and Paul Seidenstat (New Brunswick, NJ: Transaction, 1993), 113–129.

42. John C. Morris and Elizabeth D. Morris, "Privatization in Mississippi Corrections," in *Impact, Economic, Financial, and Management Analysis: For the Mississippi Department of Corrections* (Mississippi State: The John C. Stennis Institute of Government, 1997), Chap. 5.

43. See AFSCME, "The Evidence Is Clear."

44. See John D. Donahue, *The Privatization Decision: Public Ends, Private Means* (New York: Basic Books, 1989), 32.

45. Ibid.

46. Ibid.

47. Ibid., 22.

48. Madsen Pirie, *Dismantling the State* (Dallas: National Center for Policy Analysis, 1985). Offers a representative summary of the British approach to privatization.

49. See Donahue, *The Privatization Decision*, 39.

50. Stuart M. Butler, *Privatizing Federal Spending: A Strategy to Eliminate the Deficit* (New York: Universe Books, 1985), 1–186.

51. Morris and Morris, "Privatization in Mississippi Corrections."

52. William T. Gormley, Jr., "The Privatization Controversy," *Privatization and Its Alternatives*, ed. William T. Gormley, Jr. (Madison: The University of Wisconsin Press, 1991), 3–16.

53. Ibid.

54. Ibid.

55. James Austin and Garry Coventry, *Emerging Issues on Privatized Prisons* (Washington, DC: National Council on Crime and Delinquency, Bureau of Justice Assistance, Office of Justice Programs, U.S. Department of Justice, February 2001), 1.

56. Ibid, 2.

57. Moe, "Exploring the Limits," 453–60.

58. Ibid.

59. See Deborah A. Auger, "Privatization, Contracting, and States: Lessons From State Government Experience," *Public Productivity & Management Review* 22, no. 4 (June 1999): 435–454.

60. See McDonald, Fournier, Russell-Einhorn, and Crawford, *Private Prisons in the United States*, 53.

61. Jan M. Chaiken and Stephen T. Mennemeyer, *Lease-purchase Financing of Prison and Jail Construction* (Washington, DC: U.S. Department of Justice, National Institute of Justice, Office of Communication and Research Utilization, 1987), 1–32.

62. E. S. Savas, "Policy Analysis for Local Government: Public vs. Private Refuse Collection," *Policy Analysis* 3, no. 1 (1977): 49–74.

63. See Auger, "Privatization, Contracting, and States," 435–454.

64. Ibid.

65. A. Walker, "The Political Economy of Privatization," *Privatisation and the Welfare State*, eds. Julian Legrand and Ray Robinson (London: Allen & Unwin, 1984), 19–44.

66. Ibid., 19.

67. David Jackson, "Broken Teens in Correctional Facilities Left in Wake of Private Gains," *Knight-Ridder/Business Tribune News*, September 27, 1999; Frederick C. Thayer, "Privatization: Carnage, Chaos, and Corruption," *Private Means Public Ends: Private Business in Social Service Delivery*, eds. Barry J. Carroll, Ralph W. Conant and Thomas A. Easton (New York: Praeger, 1987), 1–204; Dennis J. Palumbo, "Privatization and Corrections Policy," *Policy Studies Review* 5, no. 3 (1986): 598–606; Dennis J. Palumbo and James R. Maupin, "The Political Side of Privatization," *The Journal of Management Science and Policy Analysis* 6, no. 2 (1989): 24–40; Ira Robbins, "Privatization of Corrections: Defining the Issues," *Judicature* 69, no. 6 (1986): 325–331; Paul Starr, "The Limits of Privatization," *Prospects for Privatization*, ed. Steve H. Hanke (New York: Academy of Political Science, 1987).

68. Michael Hansen, *Private Operations of State Prisons: An Analysis of Philosophical, Practical, and Economic Concerns* (Lansing, February 1997), http://www.senate .michigan.gov/sfa/Publications/Issues/PRIVPRIS/PRIVPRIS.html.

69. Jonathan Cohn, "America's Abu Ghraibs: Abroad at Home," *The New Republic Online*, May 24, 2004, http://www.tnr.com/doc.mhtml?pt=afs%2F9kV2Z8Rvs EQdkEEPwR%3D%3D.

70. John C. Morris, *Government and Market Pathologies of Privatization: The Case of Prison Privatization* (Mississippi State, MS: Stennis Institute of Government, 1999).

71. Ibid.

72. Starr, "The Limits of Privatization."

73. Ibid.

74. Jackson, "Broken Teens"; Thayer, "Privatization"; Palumbo, "Privatization and Corrections Policy," 598–606; Palumbo and Maupin, "The Political Side of Privatization," 24–40; Robbins, "Privatization of Corrections," 325–331; Starr, "The Limits of Privatization."

75. Nicholas Henry, "The Contracting Conundrum in the United States: Or, Do We Really Understand Privatization?" *Privatization or Public Enterprise Reform? International Case Studies with Implications for Public Management*, ed. Ali Farazmand (Westport, CT: Greenwood, 2001).

76. Allen J. Beck and Paige M. Harrison, "Prisoners in 2000," *Bureau of Justice Statistics Bulletin* NCJ-188207 (August 2001): 1.

77. Ibid.

Chapter Two

1. See Eric Montague, *Private Prisons: A Sensible Solution* (Seattle, WA: Washington Policy Center, August 2001), http://www.washingtonpolicy.org/ConOut Privatization/PBMontagueCOPrivatePrisons.html.

2. See Shichor, *Punishment for Profit*, 45.

3. John P. McKay, Bennett D. Hill, and John Buckler. *A History of Western Society* (Boston: Houghton-Mifflin, 1983), 45.

4. Linowes, *Privatization*, quoted in Sichor, *Punishment for Profit*, 1.

5. See G. J. Mueller, *Public Choice* (Cambridge: Sage, 1992), 391–415.

6. See James T. Bennett, and Thomas J. DiLorenzo, "Public Employee Unions and the Privatization of Public Services," *Journal of Labor Research* 4 (1983): 33–45.

7. John J. DiIulio, Jr., "What's Wrong with Private Prisons," *Public Interest* 92 (Summer 1988): 66-83.

8. Charles B. DeWitt, "New Construction Methods for Correctional Facilities," *Construction Bulletin: National Institute of Justice* (Washington, DC: U.S. Department of Justice, 1986), J28.3/2:C76. http://www.ojp.usdoj.gov/nij/.

9. Segal and Moore, *Weighing the Watchman*, 17.

10. Charles Logan and Bill W. McGriff, "Comparing Costs of Public and Private Prisons: A Case Study" (Washington, DC: National Institute of Justice Reports, 1989), 216.

11. Wayne H. Calabrese, "Low Cost, High Quality, Good Fit: Why Not Privatization," *Privatizing Correctional Institutions*, eds. Gary W. Bowman, Simon Hakim, and Paul Seidenstat (New Brunswick, NJ: Transaction, 1993).

12. U.S. General Accounting Office (GAO). *Private and Public Prison: Studies Comparing Operational Costs and/or Quality of Service* (Washington, DC: U.S. General Accounting Office, August 1996), 6, http://www.gao.gov/archive/1996/gg96158 .pdf.

13. Ibid.

14. Ibid.

15. Ibid.

16. Segal and Moore, *Weighing the Watchman*, 17.

17. Ibid.

18. J. Stergois, "State is Prisoner of Outdated System," *Boston Herald—Op-Ed*, September 17, 2001, 35.

19. Ibid.

20. Ibid.

21. Ibid.

22. See Criminal Justice Institute, "Prison Populations," *The Corrections Yearbook* (Washington, DC: CJI, 2000), 3.

23. Stergois, "State is Prisoner," 35.
24. Ibid.
25. See Criminal Justice Institute, "Prison Populations," 3.
26. Ibid.
27. Ibid.
28. Paul Guppy, *Private Prisons and the Public Interest: Improving Quality and Reducing Cost through Competition* (Seattle, WA: Washington Policy Center, February 2003), http://www.washingtonpolicy.org/ConOutPrivatization/PNPrisonsPublicInterest 03-06.html.
29. Ibid., 1.
30. Moore, *Private Prisons*.
31. See Montague, *Private Prisons*.
32. Segal and Moore, *Weighing the Watchman*, 17.
33. Ibid.
34. Cunningham, "Public Strategies."
35. Levinson, "Okeechobee," *The Prison Journal* 65, no. 2 (Autumn/Winter 1985): 91.
36. Ibid.
37. Brian Dawe, Gary Harkins, and Lance Corcoran, *An Analysis of the Issues* (Corrections USA, February 20, 2003), http://www.azcops.org/article_6.html.
38. Ibid.
39. Ibid.
40. Bates, "Prisons for Profit," 8–11.
41. Ibid.
42. AFSCME, "The Evidence Is Clear."
43. Ibid.
44. Ibid.
45. Dawe, Harkins, and Corcoran, *An Analysis of the Issues*.
46. Office of Program Policy Analysis and Government Accountability (OPPAGA), *Private Prison Review: South Bay Correctional Facility Provides Savings and Success; Room for Improvement* (Tallahassee, FL: OPPAGA, March 2000), Report 99-39.
47. See American Federation of State County and Municipal Employees (AFSCME), "Hidden Costs Boost Corporate Profits But Increase Taxpayers' Costs," AFSCME (2003), http://www.afscme.org/private/crimep03.htm.
48. Ibid.
49. Jeremy Quittner, "The Incarceration Industry: Teeming Prison Rolls Bode Well for Private Jails," Fox News, April 22, 1998, http://www.prisonactivist.org/news/5-98/The-Incarceration-Industry-Teeming-Prison.html.
50. Joel Dyer, *The Perpetual Prisoner Machine: How America Profits from Crime* (Boulder: Westview, 2000), 217.

51. Ibid.

52. DiIulio, "What's Wrong with Private Prisons," 66–83.

53. American Federation of State County and Municipal Employees (AFSCME), "The Record—For-Profit Private Prisons Do Not Provide Measurable Costs Savings," AFSCME (2004), http://www.afscme.org/private/evid04.htm.

54. Ibid.

55. Ibid.

56. Ibid.

57. Ibid.

58. Ibid.

59. Lou Fecteau, "Audit: Hobbs Prison Deficient," *Albuquerque Journal,* June 16, 1999: A1.

60. Ibid.

61. R. Locker, "Prison Officials Defend Procedures at Mason," *The Commercial Appeal,* Memphis, July 9, 1999: A1.

62. AFSCME, "The Record."

63. Paul Wade, "CCA OK'd to Run 2 More Years," *The Commercial Appeal,* Memphis, December 10, 1999: B1.

64. Ibid.

65. Ibid.

66. AFSCME, "The Record."

67. See Lawrence L. Martin, "A Proposed Methodology for Comparing the Costs of Government versus Contract Service Delivery," *The Municipal Yearbook* (Washington, DC: ICMA, 1992), 12–15.

68. AFSCME, "The Record."

69. Ibid.

70. Mark Oswald, "Wackenhut Billing N. M. For Empty Beds," *The New Mexican,* September 9, 1999, quoted in AFSCME, "The Evidence Is Clear."

71. Ibid.

72. Ibid.

73. Richard W. Harding, *Private Prisons and Public Accountability* (New Brunswick, NJ: Transaction, 1997), 14.

74. AFSCME, "The Record."

75. Cindy Horswell, "Private Prison Firm Pulling out after Dispute with School District," *Houston Chronicle,* September 3, 1998: 32.

76. Mark Wiebe, "Detention Center Meets Opposition in Push to Change Classification," *The Kansas City Star,* March 12, 1998: 1.

77. AFSCME, "The Record."

78. "Divided Wiggins Votes Today on Private Prison Plan," *Denver Post,* July 8, 1997, B04. Quoted in AFSCME, "The Evidence Is Clear."

79. National Conference of State Legislatures (NCSL), *State Crime Legislation: 1988* 23, no. 19 (November 1988): 13.

Notes

80. Todd Mason, "It's a Bust: Many for-Profit Jails Hold No Profits—nor Even Any Inmates; Still Promoters Keep Pushing Privately Run Prisons to Job-Hungry Towns; Texas Rent-a-Cell Breakout," *The Wall Street Journal*, June 18, 1991, A1.

81. "State Liable in Suits by Cons in Private Prisons," *Associated Press*, October 13, 1999.

82. Cheryl W. Thompson, "D.C. Sues Private Prison Firm in Contract Dispute: CCA Failed to Protect and Defend the City in Two Lawsuits, Complaint Contends," *The Washington Post*, December 19, 1998: B07.

83. Cornell Corrections Inc. Form S-3, Securities and Exchange Commission. Washington, DC, Cornell Corrections Inc., November 18, 1999.

84. Howard P. Sompayrac, Jr., "Tennessee County Finds in Private in Private Prison," *The Phoenix Gazette*, April 7, 1990: A15.

85. Richardson v. McKnight; see the Oyez Web site: http://www.oyez.org/oyez/resource/case/1414/.

86. Ibid.

87. Joseph Neff, "Lawmakers Want To Let A Private-Prison Company Double The Capacity of the Facilities It Is Building," *News and Observer*, February 6, 1998, http://www.newsobserver.com.

88. Bates, "Prisons for Profit," 8–11.

89. AFSCME, "The Record."

90. Ibid.

91. Ziva Branstetter, "Avalon Doesn't Notice Inmate Gone for a Day," *Tulsa World*, June 24, 2004, http://www.pscoa.org/privatization/june%2004/29.htm.

92. Lonn Kaduce-Lanza and Karen Parker, *A Comparative Recidivism Analysis of Releasees from Private and Public Prisons in Florida* (Tallahassee, FL: Florida Correctional Privatization Commission, 1998).

93. Gilbert Geis, Alan Mobeley, and David Shichor, "Private Prisons, Criminological Research, and Conflict of Interest: A Case Study," *Crime and Delinquency*, 45, no. 3 (July 1999), 372–388. http://cad.sagepub.com/cgi/content/abstract/45/3/372.

94. Ibid.

95. Ibid.

96. Ibid.

97. Ibid.

98. Ibid.

99. Jackson, "Broken Teens."

100. R. G. Dunlop, "Cutting Corners: Profits and Private Prisons; Speaking Softly, Carrying No Stick," *The Courier-Journal*, Louisville, KY, December 21, 1993: 01A.

101. Mark Tatge, "Panel to Address Violence at Private Prison," *The Cleveland Plain Dealer*, August 20, 1998: 5B.

102. Ibid.

103. "When Private is Public," *The Ledger*, Lakeland, FL, June 8, 1999: A6.

104. "Audit Criticizes Management of Two Private Prisons," *Associated Press* October 2, 1999.

105. AFSCME, "The Record"; "Growing Pains for 2 Prisons: Private Facilities Have Glitches, Audit Says," *The Florida Times-Union*, December 5, 1999: B-1.

106. Lou Fecteau, "Upgrades at 2 Prisons Proposed," *Albuquerque Journal*, October 22, 1999: A1.

107. AFSCME, "The Record."

108. Sue Burrell and Michael Dale, "Trading on At-Risk Kids Leaves Company Poorer, Not Wiser," *The Palm Beach Post*, September 17, 1999: 23A; Gary Kane, "Firm Was Losing Money on Pahokee Youth Prison," *The Palm Beach Post*, August 27, 1999: 7B.

109. Ardy Friedberg, "Teller County Fires Private Jail Company," *The Gazette*, Colorado Springs, August 19, 1998, A1.

110. Tom Kenworthy, "Colorado Shuts Down Private Juvenile Jail," *The Washington Post*, April 22, 1999: A03.

111. Ibid.

112. "Prison Contract Canceled," *Tulsa World*, September 27, 1997: A8.

113. Robert Tanner, "State Ends Prison Pact," *The Herald*, February 20, 1997: 1B.

114. Ibid.

115. Jim Macdonald, "Dynamics of Growth of the Privatization Industry" (paper presented at the 4th Annual Privatizing Correctional Facilities, Las Vegas, NV September 24, 1999).

116. "Private prisons bad idea for Ontario, official warns," *Daily Commercial News and Construction Record*, June 1, 2000, B16.

117. AFSCME, "The Record."

Chapter Three

1. Merriam-Webster On-line Dictionary. http://www.m-w.com/cgi-bin/dictionary?book=Dictionary&va=empirical.

2. See William D. Berry and Mitchell S. Sanders, *Understanding Multivariate Research: A Primer for Beginning Social Scientists* (Boulder, CO: Westview, 2000), 45.

3. See Barbara Ann Stolz, "Policy-making Arena and Privatization: Subgovernment in Flux?" in *Privatization in Criminal Justice: Past, Present, and Future*, ed. D. Shichor and M. J. Gilbert (Cincinnati: Anderson, 2001), 23–40; Jackson, "Broken Teens."

4. Ibid.

5. Frances Stokes Berry, "Innovation in Public Management: The Adoption of Strategic Planning," *Public Administration Review* 54, no. 4 (July/August 1994): 330–332.

6. See Michael Fix and Daphne A. Kenyon, *Coping with Mandates: What Are the Alternatives?* (Washington, DC: Urban Institute, 1990).

7. See Berry, "Innovation in Public Management," 330–332.

8. Ibid.

9. Ibid.

Notes

10. Peter W. Greenwood, "Investing in Prisons or Prevention: The State Policy Makers Dilemma," *Crime & Delinquency* 44, no. 1 (January 1998): 136–142.

11. Ibid.

12. See Bureau of Justice Statistics, "Prison and Jail Inmates 1995," *Bureau of Justice Statistics Bulletin* NCJ-161132 (1996): 1-16, http://www.ojp.usdoj.gov/bjs/pub/pdf/pji95.pdf.

13. Greenwood, "Investing in Prisons or Prevention," 136–142.

14. Ibid, 136.

15. See Jon Marc Taylor, "Praised Goals/ Misplaced Blame," *Cell Door Magazine* 5, no. 2 (December 2003), http://www.lairdcarlson.com/celldoor/00502/Taylor00502 PraisedGoalsMisplacedBlame.htm.

16. Ibid.

17. Ibid.

18. Ibid.

19. Moore, *Private Prisons*, 1.

20. Ibid, 7.

21. Corina Eckl, "The Cost of Corrections," *State Legislatures* 24, no. 2, (February 1998), http://www.questia.com/PM.qst;jsessionid=DY6VHWnRJyFyBNNzDJHjQ 216vpGSd6rcyfbGC2BrYL8Nb9z99Jpc!-859922093!-85559974?a=o&d= 5001333057.

22. Ibid.

23. Judy Zelio, "Seasons of Spending," *State Legislatures*, July/August 1999, http://www.ncsl.org/programs/pubs/799spend.htm.

24. See James Stephen, "State Prison Expenditures, 2001," *Bureau of Justice Statistics Special Report* NCJ-202949 (June 2004), http://www.ojp.usdoj.gov/bjs/pub/pdf/spe01.pdf.

25. Ibid.

26. Virginia Gray, "The Socioeconomic and Political Context of States," in *Politics in the American States 7th edition: A Comparative Analysis,* eds. Virginia Gray and Herbert Jacob (Washington, DC: CQ Press, 1996), 1–34.

27. Ibid.

28. See Arthur N. Dunning, James G. Ledbetter, and Joseph Whorton of the Carl Vinson Institute of Government, *Dismantling Persistent Poverty: In the Southeastern States, 2002,* http://www.cviog.uga.edu.

29. Ibid.

30. See Steven D. Gold, *Measuring Fiscal Effort and Fiscal Capacity: Sorting Out Some of the Controversies*) (Boston, MA: Oelgeschlager, Gunn, & Hain in association with the Lincoln Institute of Land Policy, 1986), 29–50.

31. Ibid.

32. Advisory Commission on Intergovernmental Relations (ACIR), *Tax Capacity of the Fifty States* (Washington, DC: U. S. Government Printing Office, 1982), 2.

33. Robert D. Plotnick and Richard D. Winters, "A Politico-Economic Theory of Income Redistribution," *American Political Science Review* 79 (1985): 458–473;

Frances Stokes Berry and William D. Berry, "Tax Innovation in the States: Capitalizing on Political Opportunity," *American Journal of Political Science* 36 (1992): 715–742.

34. Robert Tannenwald and Jonathan Cowan, "Fiscal Capacity, Fiscal Need, and Fiscal Comfort among U.S. States: New Evidence," *Publius: The Journal of Federalism* 27 no. 3 (Summer 1997), http://www.bos.frb.org/economic/econbios/tannenwa.htm.

35. See Gold, *Measuring Fiscal Effort*, 29–50.

36. Ibid.

37. Robert Tannenwald, "Fiscal Disparity Among the States Revisited," *New England Economic Review*, July/August 1999, 1–23, http://www.bos.frb.org/economic/neer/neer1999/neer499a.pdf.

38. Ira Sharkansky, "Economic and Political Correlates of State Government Expenditures: General Tendencies and Deviant Cases," *Midwest Journal of Political Science* 11, no. 2 (May 1967): 173–192.

39. Yaw Agyeman Badu and Sheng Yung Li, "Fiscal Stress in Local Government: A Case Study of the Tri-Cities in the Commonwealth of Virginia," *Review of Black Political Economy* 22, no. 3 (Winter 1994): 5–18.

40. Ibid, 7.

41. George Wolohojan, Irene Rubin, and Charles Levine, *The Politics of Retrenchment: How Local Governments Manage Fiscal Stress* (Beverly, Hills: Sage, 1981), 224.

42. Badu and Li, "Fiscal Stress in Local Government," 5–18.

43. Edward Bender, "A Contributing Influence: The Private-Prison Industry and Political Giving in the South," The Institute on Money in State Politics, http://www.followthemoney.org.

44. See Paula Wade and R. Locker, Not So Fast, Naifeh Says of Prison Switch Over. *The Commercial Appeal*, Memphis, February 18, 1996: A1.

45. Bender, "A Contributing Influence."

46. Ibid.

47. Ibid.

48. See Amy Cheung, *Prison Privatization and the Use of Incarceration* (briefing sheet, the Sentencing Project, September 2004), 4, http://www.sentencingproject.org/order.

49. Ibid, 4–5.

50. Ibid, 5.

51. Ibid, 5.

52. See Bridgette Sarabi, and Edward Bender, "The Prison Payoff: The Role of Politics and Private Prisons in the Incarceration Boom," *Western Prison Project*, November 2000: 4, http://www.westernstatescenter.org/archive/ppayoff.pdf.

53. See Cheung, *Prison Privatization*, 5.

54. Samuel C. Patterson, "Legislative Politics in the States," in *Politics in the American States: A Comparative Analysis*, eds. Virginia Gray and Herbert Jacob (Washington, DC: CQ Press, 1996).

55. Ibid.

56. Thad Beyle, "Governors: 1996. The Middlemen and Women in Our Political System," *Politics in the American States: A Comparative Analysis*, eds. Virginia Gray and Herbert Jacob (Washington, DC: CQ Press, 1996).

57. Ibid.

58. Patterson, "Legislative Politics," 159–206.

59. Ibid.

60. See Auger, "Privatization, Contracting, and States," 435–454.

61. Thomas M. Holdbrook-Provow and Steven C. Poe, "Measuring State Political Ideology," *American Politics Quarterly* 15, no. 3 (July 1987): 399–416.

62. Ibid.

63. Daniel Elazar, *American Federalism: A View from the States,* 3rd ed. (New York: Harper and Row, 1972).

64. Ibid.

65. Greg A. Calderia and Andrew T. Cowart, "Budgets, Institutions, and Change: Criminal Justice Policy in America," *American Journal of Political Science* 24, no. 3 (August 1980): 413–438.

66. Ibid.

67. Elazar, *American Federalism.*

68. G. Newman, *The Punishment Response* (Albany, NY: Harrow and Heston, 1985).

69. William D. Berry, Evan J. Ringquist, Richard C. Fording, and Russell L. Hanson, "Measuring Citizen and Government Ideology in the American States, 1960–93," *American Journal of Political Science* 42, no. 1 (January 1998): 335.

70. Robert S. Erickson, Gerald C. Wright, and John P. McIver, *Statehouse Democracy: Public Opinion and Policy in the American States* (Cambridge: Cambridge University Press, 1993).

71. Berry, Ringquist, Fording, and Hanson, "Measuring Citizen and Government Ideology," 335; Berry and Berry, "Tax Innovation in the States," 715–742; Robert D. Brown, "Party Cleavages and Welfare Effort in the American States," *American Political Science Review* 89 (1995): 23–33; Plotnick and Winters, "A Politico-Economic Theory," 458–473; Berry and Berry, "Tax Innovation in the States," 715–742.

72. See Stolz, "Policy-making Arena and Privatization," 23–40; Jackson, "Broken Teens."

73. Irwin and Austin, *It's About Time.*

74. Ibid, 78.

75. Ibid.

76. Ibid.

77. Irwin and Austin, *It's About Time.*

78. Marsha Rosenbaum, *Just Say What?* (San Francisco: National Council on Crime and Delinquency, 1989), 67.

79. Irwin and Austin, *It's About Time.*

80. Gray, "Innovation in the States," 1174–85; Irwin Feller and Donald C. Menzel. "The Adoption of Technological Innovations by Municipal Governments," *Urban Affairs Quarterly* 13 (1978): 469–489.

81. Jack L. Walker, "The Diffusion of Innovation among the States," *American Political Science Review* 68 (September 1969): 880–899.

82. Frances Stokes Berry and William D. Berry, "State Lottery Adoptions as Policy Innovations: An Event History Analysis," *American Political Science Review* 84, no. 2 (June 1990): 395–415.

83. Ibid.

84. Berry and Berry, "State Lottery Adoptions," 395–415.

85. Ira Sharkansky, *Regionalism in American Politics* (New York: Bobbs-Merrill, 1970); Fred W. Grupp and Alan R. Richards, "Variations in Elite Perceptions of American States as Referents for Public Policy Making," *American Political Science Review* 69, no. 3 (September 1975): 850–58; Patricia K. Freeman, "Interstate Communication among State Legislators Regarding Energy Policy Innovations," *Publius* 15 (Fall 1985): 99–111; Alfred R. Light, "Intergovernmental Sources of Innovation in State Administration," *American Politics Quarterly* 6, no. 2 (April 1978): 147–166.

86. Berry and Berry, "State Lottery Adoptions," 395–415.

87. Berry, "Innovation in Public Management," 330–332; Sharkansky, *Regionalism*; Elazar, *American Federalism*.

88. Elazar, *American Federalism*, 109.

89. Jody L. Fitzpatrick and Rodney E. Hero, "Political Culture and Political Characteristics of the American States: A Consideration of Some Old and New Questions," *Western Political Quarterly* 41, no. 1 (March 1988): 145–153.

90. Ibid.

91. Robert S. Erickson, John P. McIver, and Gerald C. Wright, "State Political Culture and Public Opinion," *American Political Science Review* 81, no. 3 (September 1987): 9.

92. Ibid.

93. Ibid.

94. "The Issues: Prison Overcrowding," *CQ Researcher* 4, no. 5 (February 1994): 25.

95. William H. Rehnquist, Speech to National Symposium on Drugs and Violence in America, June 1993. Cited in David B. Kopel, "Prison Blues: How America's Foolish Sentencing Policies Endanger Public Safety," *Cato Policy Analysis No. 208,* https://www.cato.org/pubs/pas/pa-208.html.

96. Curtis R. Blakely and Vic W. Bumphus, "Private Correctional Management: A Comparison of Enabling Legislation," *Federal Probation,* 60, no. 2 (June 1996): 49–54.

97. See T. L. Snell, "Correctional Populations in the United States," *Bureau of Justice Statistics Bulletin* NCJ-146413.

98. "The Issues: Prison Overcrowding," 25.

99. Darrell K. Gilliard and Allen J. Beck, "Prisoners in 1997," *Bureau of Justice Statistics Bulletin* NCJ 1700 14 (August 1998), 2, 9.

100. "The Issues: Prison Overcrowding."

101. David B. Kopel, "Prison Blues: How America's Foolish Sentencing Policies Endanger Public Safety," *Cato Policy Analysis No. 208,* https://www.cato.org/pubs/pas/pa-208.html.

102. Matt Grayson, "Laying Down the Law: Study Claims Mandatory Minimums Cost Maximum Dollars," *Spectrum: The Journal of State Government* 70, no. 3 (Summer 1997): 2–4.

103. See *Florida News-Sentinel,* 1997, A1.

104. Yijia Jing, "State Prison Privatization in the US: A Study of the Causes and Magnitude" (doctoral dissertation, Ohio State University, August 2005).

105. Ibid.

Chapter Four

1. See Mattera and Khan, *Jail Breaks,* v.

2. DeWitt, "New Construction Methods."

3. William C. Collins, *Privately Operated Speculative Prisons and Public Safety: A Discussion of Issues* (Washington, D.C.: Corrections Program Office, Office of Justice Programs, United States Department of Justice), 3.

4. Christopher Swope, "The Inmate," *Governing,* October 1998: 19.

5. McDonald, Patten, Fournier, and Crawford, *Government's Management,* 6.

6. Ibid.

7. McDonald, Patten, Fournier, and Crawford, *Government's Management.*

8. Bender, "A Contributing Influence."

9. "Privatizing Prisons," Center for Policy Alternatives, http://www.cfpa.org/issues/issue.cfm/issue/PrivatizingPrisons.xml.

10. Jeanne B. Stinchcomb, "Current Trends and Future Issues," in *Corrections: Past, Present, and Future* (Lanham, MD: The American Correctional Association, 2005), 56.

11. Collins, *Privately Operated,* Appendix A.

12. AFSCME, "The Record."

13. Ibid, 3.

14. Ibid, 3.

15. "State Liable."

16. AFSCME, "The Record."

17. Thompson, "D.C. Sues," B07; AFSCME, "The Record."

18. Cornell Corrections Inc. Form S-3, Securities and Exchange Commission. Washington, DC, Cornell Corrections Inc., November 18, 1999.

19. Sompayrac, "Tennessee County Finds Pitfalls," A15.

20. Collins, *Privately Operated,* 3.

21. Ibid.

Chapter Five

1. James A. Caporaso and David Levine, *Theories of Political Economy* (New York: Cambridge University Press, 2000), 7.

2. Prison Law Project of the National Lawyers Guild, *Crime and Prisons*, Fall 1994. Cited in the *San Diego Union Tribune Op-ed*, December 4, 1995.

3. South West Regional Assembly, "South West Definition of Social Exclusion," *Social Inclusion and Equalities*, http://www.southwest-ra.gov.uk/swra/ourwork/equalities/index.shtml.

4. Willie Wisely, "The Bottom Line: California's Prison Industrial Authority," Update: California's expanding prison-industrial complex, Prison Activist Resource Center, 2002, http://www.prisonactivist.org/crisis/prison-industrial.html.

5. Ibid.

6. Grassroots Leadership, "Education v. Incarceration: A Mississippi Case Study," Grassroots Leadership homepage, http://www.grassrootsleadership.org/downloads/miss_3.pdf.

7. Ibid.

8. Ibid.

9. Ibid.

10. Greg Godwin,"Prisons and Profits," *People's Weekly World Newspaper*, November 10, 2001, http://www.pww.org/article/articleview/139/1/21.

11. Ibid.

12. Michael Tonry and Joan Petersilia, "Prison Research at the Beginning of the 21st Century," in *Prisons*, eds. Michael Tonry and Joan Petersilia (Chicago: University of Chicago Press, 1999), 11.

13. Eric Lotke, "New Growth Industries: The Prison Industrial Complex," *Multinational Monitor* 17, no. 11 (November 1996), http://multinationalmonitor.org/hyper/mm1196.06.html.

14. Lynn Schmaltz, "[Prison Act] Owners of Prison System in America," 100777.com (September 2004), http://100777.com/node/1318.

15. Karyl K. Kicenski, *The Corporation Prison: The Production of Crime & the Sale of Discipline: A Proposal to Study the Drive to Privatize the Prison System in the State of California* (April 2002), 2, http://www.csun.edu/~hfspc002/karyl.prison.pdf.

16. Ibid., 2.

17. Solari Action Network, *Soros Report on Prison Financing*, March 14, 2003. Discussion board. http://www.solariactionnetwork.com/phpBB2/viewtopic.php?p=7293&highlight=&; Mattera and Khan, *Jail Breaks*, 14.

18. Ibid., 14.

19. Ibid., 14.

20. Graham Boyd, "The Drug War Is the New Jim Crow," *NACLA Report on the Americas*, July/August 2001: 3.

21. Ibid.

Notes

22. Camille Graham Camp and George M. Camp, "The 2000 Corrections Yearbook: Private Prisons, Criminal Justice Institute," in *The Corrections Yearbook* (Middletown, CT: CJI, 2000), 109.

23. Paige M. Harrison and Jennifer C. Karberg, "Prison and Jail Inmates at Midyear 2003," *Bureau of Justice Statistics Bulletin*, July 14, 2004. http://www.ojp.usdoj .gov/bjs/abstract/p03.htm

24. Ibid.

25. Frank T. Flynn, "The Federal Government and the Prison Labor Problem in the States" (dissertation, University of Chicago, 1949), http://wwwlib.umi.com/ dissertations/results?set_num=1.

26. Ibid., 4; U.S. Bureau of Labor Statistics,. *Prison Labor in the United States*, 4, 1940.

27. Flynn, "The Federal Government," 30; U.S. Bureau of Labor Statistics, *Prison Labor in the United States*, 4.

28. Ibid.

29. Ibid.

30. Ibid.

31. Deloitte and Touche, Executive Summary, "Independent Market Study of UNI-COR Federal Prison Industries, Inc," DRT International, Washington: Report to Congress on Study Findings and Recommendations. 65, 1991.

32. Dianne C. Dwyer and Rogers B. McNally, "Public Policy, Prison Industries, and Business: An Equitable Balance for 1990s," *Federal Probation* 57, no. 2 (June 1993), http://www.uscourts.gov/library/fpcontents.html.

33. R. C. Grieser, *The Economic Impact of Cocraft Correctional Industries in New York State* (Alexandria, VA: Institute for Economic and Policy Studies, 1988), 1.

34. Anna Mundow, "The Business of Prisons," *Greater Diversity News*, http://www .greaterdiversity.com/employers/emp_articles03/Business_Prison.html.

35. Grieser, *The Economic Impact.*

36. Ibid.

37. Dwyer and McNally, "Public Policy."

38. Federal Bureau of Prisons, "UNICOR: Federal Prison Industries, Inc.," Federal Bureau of Prisons, http://www.bop.gov/inmate_programs/unicor.jsp.

39. DC Dave. "Statement to US House," The Home Page of DC Dave, http://www .dcdave.com/article1/080598.html.

40. Federal Bureau of Prisons, "UNICOR."

41. Ibid.

42. Rosalind P. Petchesky, "At Hard Labor: Penal Confinement and Production in Nineteenth-Century America," in *Crime and Capitalism*, ed. David F. Greenberg (Alto, CA: Mayfield, 1981), 341–57.

43. Ibid., 341.

44. Ibid., 342.

45. A copy of this article can be found at the Real Cost of Prisons Weblog, "No Surprise! Race a factor in job offers for African American men who have been incarcerated," http://realcostofprisons.org/blog/archives/2005/06/no_surprise _rac.html.

46. Mattera and Khan, *Jail Breaks*, 28.

47. Tracy L. Huling, "Prisons as a Growth Industry in Rural America: An Exploratory Discussion on the Effects of Young African Men in the Inner Cities, A Consultation of the United States Comission on Civil Rights," *Rural Development Perspectives*, April 1999: 4.

48. Calvin Beale, "Rural Prisons: An Update," *Rural Development Perspectives* 11, no. 2 (February 1996): 2.

49. Jackson, "Broken Teens."

50. Bender. "A Contributing Influence."

51. Beck and Harrison, "Prisoners in 2000."

52. Bender. "A Contributing Influence."

53. David Shichor, "Private Prisons in Perspective: Some Conceptual Issues," *The Howard Journal*, 37, no. 1 (February 1998), http://www.blackwell-synergy.com/doi/abs/10.1111/1468-2311.00079

54. Bender, "A Contributing Influence," 5.

55. Amy Driscoll, "UF Prof Who Touted Private Prisons Admits Firm Paid Him," *Miami Herald*, April 27, 1999, 1.

56. Ibid., 1.

57. John Cheves, "DeLay Accepted $100,000 from Company for Charity," *Lexington Herald-Leader* 2004, 1, http://www.prisontalk.com/forums/archive/index.php/t-92521.html.

58. Sarabi and Bender, "The Prison Payoff," 4.

59. John Biewen, "Part 1: Corporate-Sponsored Crime Laws," Corrections, Inc., American RadioWorks, April 2002, http://www.americanradioworks.org/features/corrections/index.html.

60. Sarabi and Bender, "The Prison Payoff," 4.

61. Ibid., 3; American Legislative Exchange Council (ALEC), "Alec Members Scorecard for 1999 Legislative Session," ALEC newsletter, 1, no. 5 (September 1999).

62. John Biewen, "Part 1: Corporate-Sponsored Crime Laws."

63. Randall G. Shelden, "Cashing in on Crime: The Prison Industrial Complex," Shelden Says, http://www.sheldensays.com/cashing_in_on_crime.htm.

64. Ibid.

65. Randall G. Shelden, "The Prison Industrial Complex," *The Progressive Populist* 5, No. 11 (November 1, 1999): 3, http://www.populist.com/99.11.prison.html.

66. Ibid.

67. Alex Freedman, "Prisoners Exploited in Name of Profit," *The Wall Street Journal* 1995. Cited in Shirin Vossoughi, "Democracy: Prop 21 Fuels Corporate Slavery While Neglecting Rehabilitation," *Daily Bruin Online*, http://www.dailybruin.ucla.edu/db/issues/00/02.08/view.vossoughi.html.

68. Polly Mann, "Private Prisons: A Growth Industry," Women Against Military Madness, http://www.worldwidewamm.org/newsletters/2000/0600newsletter/PrivatePrisons.html.

69. J. Robert Lilly and Mathieu Deflem, "Profit and Penalty: An Analysis of the Corrections Commercial Complex," *Crime and Delinquency* 42, no. 1 (January 1996), 3–20.

70. Tracy L. Huling, "Prisoners of the Census," *Mother Jones*, May 10, 2000, http://www.motherjones.com/commentary/columns/2000/05/census.html.

71. Peter Wagner, "Importing Constituents: Prisoners and Political Clout in New York," *Prison Policy Initiative*, April 22, 2002, http://www.prisonpolicy.org/importing/importing.shtml.

72. Ibid.

73. Fox Butterfield, "Study Tracks Boom in Prisons and Notes Impact on Counties," *New York Times*, April 30, 2004: A19.

74. Boyd, "The Drug War," 20.

75. Ibid., 20.

76. Jon Kyl, "Congress Must Fix Discrimination of Non Voting by Prison Inmates," *Coolidge (AZ) News*, August 11, 2004, 1.

77. Graham Boyd, "Collateral Damage in the War on Drugs,": *Villanova Law Review* 47 (2002); available at http://www.aclu.org/drugpolicy/gen/10835pub20020501.html

78. Ibid., 5.

79. Ibid.

80. Devah Pager, "The Mark of a Criminal Record," *American Journal of Sociology* 108, No. 5 (March 2003): 975, http://www.northwestern.edu/ipr/publications/papers/2002/WP-02-37.pdf.

81. Ibid., 958.

82. See the 1998 Amendments to the Higher Education Act of 1965, P.L. 105-244; Boyd, "Collateral Damage," 839–850.

83. Christopher Mascharka, "Mandatory Minimum Sentences: Exemplifying the Law of Unintended Consequences," *Florida State University Law Review* 28, no. 4 (Summer 2001), http://www.law.fsu.edu/journals/lawreview/backissues/vol28/issue4.html. According to this article, "while 76 percent of drug users are white, African American comprise 35 percent of all drug arrests, 55 percent of all drug convictions, and 74 percent of all drug sentences."

84. See the 1998 Amendments to the Higher Education Act of 1965, P.L. 105-244. The sentencing guidelines were amended, but it does not address murder or rape as exclusionary criteria.

85. U.S. Department of Education, *The Student Guide to Financial Aid* (Washington, D.C.: U.S. Government Printing Office), 7, http://studentaid.ed.gov/students/attachments/siteresources/StudentGuideEnglish2004_05.pdf; see also http://studentaid.ed.gov/PORTALSWebApp/students/english/preparing.jsp?tab=preparing.

Chapter Six

1. Allen J. Beck and Jennifer C. Karberg, *Prison and Jail Inmates at Midyear 2000* (Washington, DC: Bureau of Justice Statistics, U.S. Department of Justice, March 2000), 4; Allen J. Beck, Jennifer C. Karberg, and Paige M. Harrison, *Prison and Jail Inmates at Midyear 2001* (Washington, DC: Bureau of Justice Statistics, U.S. Department of Justice, April 2001), 4; Paige M. Harrison and Jennifer C. Karberg, *Prison and Jail Inmates at Midyear 2002* (Washington, DC: Bureau of Justice Statistics, U.S. Department of Justice, April 2003), 4; Paige M. Harrison, and Jennifer C. Karberg, *Prison and Jail Inmates at Midyear 2003* (Washington, DC: Bureau of Justice Statistics, U.S. Department of Justice, May 2004), 4.

2. David Crary, "Private Prisons Experience Business Surge," *Associated Press*, July 30, 2005.

3. Ibid.

4. "*Know Your Rights: Medical Care for Prisoners*," American Civil Liberties Union, November 13, 2003, http://www.aclu.org/Prisons/Prisons.cfm?ID=14377&c=123.

5. Marguerite G. Rosenthal, "Prescription for Disaster: Commercialization Prison Health Care in South Carolina," Grassroots Leadership and South Carolina Fair Share, April 12, 2004: 4, http://www.soros.org/initiatives/justice/articles_publications/publications/gl_prescription_20040412/PrescriptionforDisaster.pdf.

6. Paul von Zielbauer and Joseph Planbect, "As Health Care in Jail Goes Private, 10 Days Can Be a Death Sentence," *New York Times*, April 27, 2005, http://www.nytimes.com/2005/02/27/nyregion/27jail.html?ex=1134622800&en=4742292a59d3a09f&ei=5070.

7. Ibid.

8. Ibid.

9. Mark Martin, "Scathing Report on Prison Health Care Still Not Out: Agency Suggests Negligence in Deaths at Corcoran Facility," *Chronicle Sacramento Bureau*, February 26, 2004, http://www.sfgate.com/cgi-bin/article.cgi?file=/chronicle/archive/2004/02/26/MNG2P58ILF1.DTL.

10. Fox Butterfield, "With Cash Tight, States Reassess Long Jail Terms," *New York Times*, November 10, 2003, http://www.ednotinc.org/News/TINYT.pdf.

11. Criminal Justice Institute, "Public and Private Prisons Compared," *The Corrections Yearbook: Private Prisons* (Washington, DC: CJI, 2000).

12. Shelley Rice, "The Economic Motivations of Prison Privatization: Assessing Convict Labors Influence on the Drive to Privatize Prisons" (thesis, Rutgers University, 2005), 183.

13. Ibid., 184.

Bibliography

Archambeault, William G., and Donald R. Deis. *Cost Effectiveness Comparison of Private vs. Public Prisons in Louisiana: A Comprehensive Analysis of Allen, Avoyelles, and Win Correctional Centers.* Baton Rouge: Department of Accounting, Louisiana State University, October 15, 1996.

Arizona Department of Corrections. *Public-Private Prison Comparison.* Phoenix, AZ: Arizona Department of Corrections, October 2000.

Auditor of Public Accounts, Commonwealth of Kentucky. *Privatization Review: Minimum Security Correctional Facilities.* Auditor of Public Accounts, Commonwealth of Kentucky, 1994. Quoted in Moore.

Culp, Richard. "Privatization of Juvenile Correctional Facilities in the U.S.: A Comparison of Conditions of Confinement in Private and Government Operated Programs." *Security Journal* 11, no. 2–3 (December 1998): 289–301.

Cunningham, Dennis. *The History of Private Prison Contracting in the Oklahoma Department of Corrections.* Oklahoma Department of Corrections, 1999. http://www.doc.state.ok.us/Private%20Prisons/PP_history.htm.

Bibliography

"Divided Wiggins Votes Today on Private-Prison Plan." *Denver Post*, July 8, 1997, B04.

Florida Office of the Auditor General. *Certification of Correctional Facility Actual Per Diem Costs Pursuant to Section 957.07, Florida Statues.* Tallahassee, FL: Florida Office of the Auditor General, November 1993.

Greene, Judith. "Comparing Private and Public Prison Services and Programs in Minnesota: Findings from Prisoner Interviews." *Current Issues in Criminal Justice* 11, no. 2 (November 1999): 202–32.

Home Office Economic Unit, United Kingdom, and Tim Wilson. "The United Kingdom Experience." Paper, Head of Contracts and Competition Group, Her Majesty's Prison Service, July 10, 1996.

Honovich, John R. "Corrections Industry Financing Options." Paper presented at the 4th Annual Privatizing Correctional Facilities, Las Vegas, NV, September 23, 1999.

Huling, Tracy L. "Prisons as a Growth Industry in Rural America: An Exploratory Discussion of the Effects on Young African-American Men in the Inner Cities." Washington, DC: U.S. Commission on Civil Rights, April 15–16, 1999.

Kentucky Department of Corrections. *Costs to Incarcerate.* Kentucky Department of Corrections, FY 1996–1997. Quoted in Segal and Moore.

Knight, K., M. L. Hiller, and D. D. Simpson. "Evaluating Corrections-Based Treatment for the Drug-Abusing Criminal Offender." *Journal of Psychoactive Drugs* 31, no. 3 (1999): 299–304.

Knight, K., and M. L. Hiller. "Community-Based Substance Abuse Treatment: A One Year Outcome Evaluation of the Dallas County Judicial Treatment Center." *Federal Probation* 61, no. 2 (1997): 61–68.

Logan, Charles H. *Well Kept: Comparing Quality of Confinement in a Public and a Private Prison.* Washington, DC: National Institute of Justice, 1991.

Bibliography

Mitchell, George A. *Controlling Prison Costs in Wisconsin*. Thiensville, WI: Wisconsin Policy Research Institute, December 1996.

Moore, Adrian T. *Private Prisons: Quality Corrections at a Lower Cost*. Policy Study No. 240, Reason Public Policy Institute. http://www.reason.org/ps240.pdf.

Rehfuss, John A. *Contracting Out in Government*. San Francisco: Jossey-Bass, 1989.

Richardson v. McKnight, 117 S.Ct. 2100, 138 L.Ed.2d 540 (1997).

Salamon, Lester M. (ed.), assisted by Michael S. Lund. *Beyond Privatization: The Tools of Government Action*. Washington, DC: The Urban Institute, 1989.

Sarabi, Brigette, and Edward Bender. *The Prison Payoff: The Role of Politics and Private Prisons in the Incarceration Boom*. Western Prison Project & Western States Center, November 2000. http://www.westernprisonproject.org/info/pub/story/450.

Savas, E. S. *Privatization: The Key to Better Government*. Chatham, NJ: Chatham House, 1987.

Segal, Geoffrey F., and Adrian T. Moore. *Weighing the Watchman: Evaluating the Costs and Benefits of Outsourcing Correctional Services: Part II: Reviewing the Literature on Costs and Quality Comparisons*. Policy Study No. 290, Reason Public Policy Institute, January 2002. http://www.reason.org/ps290.pdf.

Sellers, Martin. "Private and Public Prisons: A Comparison of Costs, Programs, and Facilities." *International Journal of Offender Therapy and Comparative Criminology* 10, no. 1 (1989): 22–27.

Sharp, John. *Information Report on Contracts for Corrections Facilities and Services, Recommendations to the Governor of Texas and Members of the Seventy-Second Legislature*. Austin, TX: Texas Sunset Advisory Commission, 1991.

———. *Breaking the Mold: New Ways to Govern Texas, Texas Performance Review*. 19–25. Austin, TX: Texas Comptroller of Public Accounts, July 1991.

177

Bibliography

State of Tennessee Legislative Fiscal Review Committee. *Cost Comparison of Correctional Centers.* Nashville, TN: State of Tennessee Legislative Fiscal Review Committee, 1995.

State of Washington Legislative Budget Office. *Department of Corrections Privatization Pre-Feasibility Study, Report 96–2.* Olympia, WA: State of Washington Legislative Budget Office, 1996.

Tatge, M. "Inspectors Question Youngstown Prison Access; Private Facility Refused to Let Some Inside." *The Cleveland Plain Dealer,* May 9, 1998, 4b.

Tennessee Legislature Select Oversight Committee on Corrections. *Comparative Evaluation of Privately Managed CCA Prison and State-Managed Prototypical Prison.* Nashville, TN: Tennessee Legislature Select Oversight Committee on Corrections, 1995.

Texas Criminal Justice Policy Council. *Limes to Limes: Comparing the Operational Costs of Juvenile and Adult Correctional Programs in Texas.* Texas Criminal Justice Policy Council, January 2001. http://www.cjpc.state.tx.us.

———. *Oranges to Oranges: Comparing the Operational Costs of Juvenile and Adult Correctional Programs in Texas.* Texas Criminal Justice Policy Council, January 1999. http://www.cjpc.state.tx.us.

———. *Apples to Apples: Comparing the Operational Costs of Juvenile and Adult Correctional Programs in Texas.* Texas Criminal Justice Policy Council, January 1997. http://www.cjpc.state.tx.us.

———. *Texas Correctional Costs Per Day, 1993–1994.* Texas Criminal Justice Policy Council, February 1995. http://www.cjpc.state.tx.us.

———. *Texas Correctional Costs 1989–1990.* Texas Criminal Justice Policy Council, January 1991. http://www.cjpc.state.tx.us.

———. *Texas Correctional Costs Per Day, 1993–1994.* Texas Criminal Justice Policy Council, March 1993. http://www.cjpc .state.tx.us.

Thomas, Charles W. *Comparing the Costs and Performance of Public and Private Prisons in Arizona.* Phoenix, AZ: Arizona Joint Legislative Committee, August 1997.

178

Bibliography

Urban Institute. *Comparison of Privately and Publicly Operated Corrections Facilities in Kentucky and Massachusetts*. Washington, DC: Urban Institute, 1989.

U.S. Department of Justice, Bureau of Justice Assistance. *Emerging Issues on Privatized Prisons*. Washington, DC: U.S. Department of Justice, Bureau of Justice Assistance, February 2001.

U.S. Department of Justice, National Institute of Corrections. *Private Sector Operation of a Correctional Institution: A Study of the Jack and Ruth Eckerd Youth Development Center, Okeechobee, FL*. Washington, DC: U.S. Department of Justice, National Institute of Corrections, 1985.

Index

Index

About the Author

BYRON EUGENE PRICE is Assistant Professor of Public Administration at Rutgers University, Newark. He is the Associate Director of the National Center for Public Productivity, Rutgers University, Newark; Editor-in-Chief, *Journal of Public Management and Social Policy*; and Case Study Editor, *Public Productivity and Management Review*. Dr. Price has co-authored two book chapters on Mississippi politics, co-authored one book chapter on privatization, and contributed three entries to the *Malcolm X Encyclopedia*. He has published in the *American Review of Public Administration*; the *International Review of Public Administration*, *Public Productivity and Management Review*; and the *PA Times*.